STEADFAST
CHRISTIANITY

A Study
— *of* —
2 Thessalonians

From the Bible-Teaching Ministry of

Charles R. Swindoll

INSIGHT FOR LIVING

Insight for Living's Bible teacher, Chuck Swindoll, has devoted his life to the clear, practical application of God's Word and His grace. A pastor at heart, Chuck has served as senior pastor to congregations in Texas, Massachusetts, and California. He currently leads Stonebriar Community Church in Frisco, Texas, but Chuck's listening audience extends far beyond a local church body. As a leading program in Christian broadcasting, *Insight for Living* airs in major Christian radio markets, through more than 2,100 outlets worldwide, in 16 languages, and to a growing webcast audience. Chuck's extensive writing ministry has also served the body of Christ worldwide, and his leadership as president and now chancellor of Dallas Theological Seminary has helped prepare and equip a new generation for ministry. Chuck and Cynthia, his partner in life and ministry, have four grown children and ten grandchildren.

Based on the outlines, charts, and transcripts of Charles R. Swindoll's sermons, the Bible study guide text was developed and written by the Pastoral Ministries Department of Insight for Living.

Editor in Chief:
Cynthia Swindoll

Study Guide Writers:
Brian Goins
Ken Gire
Bryce Klabunde
Bill Slabaugh

Senior Editor and Assistant Writer:
Wendy Peterson

Editor and Assistant Writer:
Marla Alupoaicei

Editorial Assistant:
Julie Martin

Editor:
Amy LaFuria

Typesetter:
Bob Haskins

Rights and Permissions:
The Meredith Agency

Unless otherwise identified, all Scripture references are from the New American Standard Bible © The Lockman Foundation 1960, 1962, 1963, 1968, 1971, 1972, 1973, 1975, 1977, 1995. Used by permission.

An effort has been made to locate sources and obtain permission where necessary for the quotations used in this book. In the event of any unintentional omission, a modification will gladly be incorporated in future printings.

ISBN 1-57972-442-6
Cover design: Alex Pasieka
Cover image: Francisco Cruz/SuperStock
Printed in the United States of America

CONTENTS

INTRODUCTION

Times were hard. Life was difficult. Pain from misunderstanding and prejudice was increasing. Like wounded deer in the forest, the Thessalonian Christians were living threatened lives under the gun of persecution. Affliction was the order of their day.

Knowing their need for affirmation, the great apostle Paul wrote them a brief yet potent letter of encouragement. It has been preserved down through the centuries and appears today in the Bible as 2 Thessalonians . . . a strong statement of steadfast Christianity.

Perhaps you, too, are feeling the sting of persecution. These may be difficult days for you, days in which you feel misunderstood and "on trial" by others. My sincere hope is that each one of these studies will give you a fresh boost of encouragement and much-needed strength for the day.

God's Word is just what the Physician ordered for hard times. May your faith grow, may your confidence in God increase, and may your load seem lighter as your Christianity becomes steadfast and immovable.

Charles R. Swindoll

PUTTING TRUTH
INTO ACTION

Knowledge apart from application falls short of God's desire for His children. He wants us to apply what we learn so that we will change and grow. This Bible study guide was prepared with these goals in mind. As you go through the following pages, we hope your desire to discover biblical truth will grow as your understanding of God's Word increases and that you will be encouraged to apply what you've learned.

To assist you in your study, we've included a section called **Living Insights** at the end of each lesson. These exercises will challenge you to study further and to think of specific ways to put your discoveries into action.

Each Living Insights section is followed by **Small Group Insights**. These thought-provoking questions will help you to faciliate discussion of the important concepts and principles in the chapter and apply them to your life.

On occasion a lesson is followed by a **Digging Deeper** section, which gives you additional information and resources to probe further into issues raised in that lesson.

There are many ways to use this guide—in personal devotions, group studies, discussions with friends and family, and Sunday school classes. And, of course, it's an ideal study aid when you're listening to its corresponding *Insight for Living* radio series.

To benefit most from this Bible study guide, we encourage you to consider it a spiritual journal. That's why we've included space in the Living Insights for recording your thoughts and discoveries. We hope you'll return to those sections often for review and encouragement as you continue to grow in your walk with Christ.

Insight for Living

STEADFAST

CHRISTIANITY

A Study
——— *of* ———
2 Thessalonians

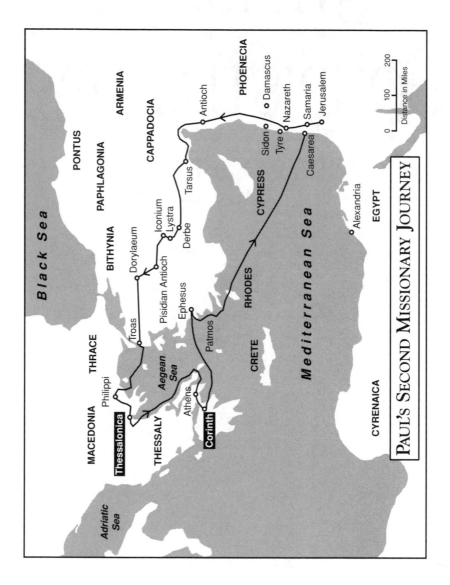

PAUL'S SECOND MISSIONARY JOURNEY

Distance in Miles

0   100   200

AN OVERVIEW OF
2 THESSALONIANS

Date of the Letter: Second Thessalonians was most likely written from Corinth in approximately A.D. 51–52.

Author: Paul

Purpose: The letter served to quell false teaching that had infiltrated the young church in Thessalonica.[1]

Brief History of Thessalonica: The city of Thessalonica is known today as Salonika and is the second largest city in Greece. It came into being in 315 B.C. Founded by the Greek general Cassander, who later became king of Macedonia, Thessalonica developed into a major commercial port and military launching point. At the time that 2 Thessalonians was written, Thessalonica was the capital and the most populous city of Macedonia, boasting over 200,000 people.[2]

During Paul's second missionary journey (A.D. 49–52), he and Silas persuaded many in this bustling seaport town to follow Christ. The city's jealous religious leaders incited a riot by bringing charges of sedition against Paul and Silas for worshipping Christ over Caesar (Acts 17:5–7). The two men were forced to flee by night to Berea (Acts 17:10).

---

1. Material on background from *Dictionary of Paul and His Letters* (Downers Grove, Ill.: InterVarsity Press, 1993), p. 933.

2. Kenneth Barker, ed., *The NIV Study Bible* (Grand Rapids, Mich.: Zondervan Publishing, 1985), p. 1819.

2 Thessalonians: Christ's Coming . . . My Response

	AFFIRMATION AMIDST AFFLICTION	EXPLANATION OF PROPHECY	CLARIFICATION REGARDING RESPONSE
	"We give thanks for you."	"Let no one deceive you."	"Now we command you."
	"We speak proudly of you."	• Mystery of Lawlessness	"If anyone does not obey . . . ."
	"We pray for you."	• Restraint Removed	"May the Lord grant peace."
		• Man of Sin	
		"So then . . . stand firm."	
	Chapter 1	**Chapter 2**	**Chapter 3**
Question	Why are we suffering?	What will occur?	How do I respond?
Contrasts	Peace amidst Pain	Lawlessness versus Restraint	Work while Waiting
Statement	"The Lord knows!"	"The day of the Lord has not yet come!"	"Do not grow weary of doing good!"
Emphasis	COMMENDATION	CORRECTION	CLARIFICATION

Writer:
Paul
(circa A.D. 51–52)

Theme:
"Hang tough!"

Key Verse:
2:15

AFFIRMING THE AFFLICTED

2 Thessalonians 1:1–4

In his book *No Greater Power*, Richard C. Halverson, former chaplain of the United States Senate, wrote:

> Crush marbles and you get fragmentation, disintegration—hard, sharp pieces. You can get hurt if you're not careful.
>
> Crush grapes and you get fragrant, refreshing wine.
>
> *Some people relate like marbles*. The fear of vulnerability hardens them. They protect themselves, allow no one to penetrate. Being vulnerable is high-risk, and they want low-risk. They bump against others and ricochet around, never enjoying a vital relationship. In brittle lovelessness, they shatter when crushed, and hurt others.
>
> *Some people relate like grapes*. They yield to pressure. They accept their weakness as essential to intimacy. They give love, knowing love is always vulnerable, knowing love is the heart and soul of our faith. When crushed, they bring blessing: fragrant, redemptive blessing.[1]

In the book of 2 Thessalonians, Paul addressed the church at Thessalonica. Like a cluster of grapes, this body of believers was caught in the winepress of persecution and affliction. Yet, as these Christians yielded to God, they began to produce a fine wine full of faith and fragrant with love, with a sweet aroma that spread to

---

1. Richard C. Halverson, *No Greater Power*, as quoted in "Affirming the Afflicted" from the Bible study guide *Steadfast Christianity*, written by Ken Gire, from the Bible teaching ministry of Charles R. Swindoll (Fullerton, Calif.: Insight for Living, 1986), p. 1.

all the churches in Asia Minor. In this letter, Paul did not focus on the "winepress" as much as he did the "wine"—the faith, love, and perseverance created as by-products of pressure.

Why Another Letter?

Most sequels lack the punch of the original. However, as the sequel to Paul's first letter to the church at Thessalonica, 2 Thessalonians swiftly dispels such a conclusion. Paul wrote:

> If anyone does not obey our instruction in this letter, take special note of that person and do not associate with him, so that he will be put to shame. (2 Thess. 3:14)

Like smelling salts, Paul's strong words grab our attention. The two letters Paul wrote to the Thessalonians must have been written within only a few months of each other—and perhaps even weeks or days. The question arises: Since Paul had just written a letter to the church, what would have prompted him to write a second letter so quickly? Undoubtedly, the second letter was written to clear up a misconception that resulted from his teaching in 1 Thessalonians 5:2–6:

> For you yourselves know full well that the day of the Lord will come just like a thief in the night. While they are saying, "Peace and safety!" then destruction will come upon them suddenly like labor pains upon a woman with child, and they will not escape. But you, brethren, are not in darkness, that the day would overtake you like a thief; for you are all sons of light and sons of day. We are not of night nor of darkness; so then let us not sleep as others do, but let us be alert and sober.

As we compare this passage with 2 Thessalonians 2:1–2, we can piece together the puzzle:

> Now we request you, brethren, with regard to the coming of our Lord Jesus Christ and our gathering together to Him, that you not be quickly shaken from your composure or be disturbed either by a spirit or a message or a letter as if from us, to the effect that the day of the Lord has come.

2

Apparently, either through a revelation someone claimed to have had, a sermon preached, or a forged document that was reputedly Paul's,[2] word had begun to spread in this church that the Day of the Lord[3] had already come. This false message produced two extreme results. Some people were "shaken" and "disturbed" (2 Thess. 2:2); others began to shirk their responsibilities, frittering away their time as they waited for the Lord's return (3:10–12).

Two practical lessons emerge from Paul's words. First, if you've been misunderstood, don't delay in trying to clear up the misunderstanding. Follow Paul's lead and be proactive in resolving the problem. Second, be certain that the information you pass on to others is clear and factual. Clarify as needed and be sure you are correctly understood. This is especially vital in spiritual matters, as Paul's experience with the Thessalonian church makes clear.

Paul's Affirmation

As we look across the landscape of Thessalonica, we see that the people were being pressed on all sides. Like soldiers on a long march, the Thessalonians were trudging through the muddy swamps of affliction. But they were no ordinary soldiers. These believers had been neither fainting in their tracks nor faltering along the roadside. Instead, they had been singing in step. But now their spirits were downcast due to a false report about the Day of the Lord. So, to bolster their spirits, Paul affirmed them with his praise. A vital principle emerges from this chapter: *Persevering through affliction develops maturity.*

Paul's Explanation

As a result of a false report or spurious letter, the Thessalonians became confused about their theology and, more specifically, their eschatology—the study of the end times. Consequently, they panicked. So Paul wrote another letter to reassure them and to help clear up their confusion.

Verses 3–12 of chapter 2 address some of the necessary ingredients that must come together before the Day of the Lord can take place: the apostasy (v. 3), the coming of the man of lawlessness

---

2. This explains Paul's personal authentication of the letter in 2 Thessalonians 3:17.

3. The *Day of the Lord* refers to the time of God's righteous intervention in history when He will mete out judgment to the nations of the earth (see Joel 1:15; 2:1–2, 31–32; Zeph. 1:14–18).

(vv. 3b–4), the removal of restraint (vv. 6–9), and the delusion of the unsaved (vv. 10–12). Later we'll study each of these terms in more depth. In verses 13–17, Paul outlined the correct response in times like these: stand firm (v. 15) and be comforted and strengthened by God (v. 17). In chapter 2, he reminded the Thessalonians that *trusting amidst confusion produces stability.*

Paul's Exhortation

On the high waves of disorienting seas, the only thing to keep a boatload of struggling saints off the reefs is a heavy anchor. In chapter 3, Paul showed the Thessalonians their anchor: "the Lord is faithful, and He will strengthen and protect you from the evil one" (v. 3). Paul prayed for the Lord to direct them and help them be steadfast (v. 5). He encouraged them to follow his responsible example (vv. 7, 9) and to not grow weary of doing good (v. 13). The unifying principle of chapter 3 is that *waiting with discipline cultivates responsibility.*

Affirmation for the Afflicted

At the time of Paul, Thessalonica stood as the most populous and prosperous city in Macedonia. In this vibrant commercial center, Christians were often treated with more than just contempt. One commentator noted, "The capital cities within the Roman Empire were the hardest places for Christians to survive, because of the fanatical intensity of emperor worship in those centers. Also . . . the young church at Thessalonica was under considerable pressure from the members of the synagogue who were opposed to the growing Christian fellowship."[4]

The Thessalonians faced a vicious, two-pronged attack—one from without and one from within. The persecution inflicted by their harassers tested their endurance; the heresy propagated by an insider chipped away at their confidence. Imagine how you would feel if you heard that you had missed the return of Christ! Your faith would be shaken and your hope for the future would dim. You might think, *I risked my life and reputation to follow the Messiah, and He has forgotten me!* What would reassure you that this was not the case? What would keep you from denying everything you believed?

---

4. Earl F. Palmer, *1 and 2 Thessalonians: A Good News Commentary,* ed. W. Ward Gasque (San Francisco, Calif.: Harper and Row, 1983), pp. 59–60.

Perhaps a letter from a trusted mentor would provide some reassurance and much-needed answers. Paul offered the believers at Thessalonica just that as he began his second letter:

> Paul and Silvanus and Timothy, to the church of the Thessalonians in God our Father and the Lord Jesus Christ: Grace to you and peace from God the Father and the Lord Jesus Christ. (2 Thess. 1:1–2)

Paul knew firsthand the afflictions faced by the fledgling church in Thessalonica. As he penned the first chapter of 2 Thessalonians, he must have remembered the rage, the insults, and the attacks from Jewish leaders who were fearful of this radical new religion (see Acts 17:4–8). Though Paul and Silas had been kicked out of Thessalonica earlier, their pupils remained. And judging from Paul's remarks, the students were receiving the same poor treatment from the Jewish community as their teachers had:

> We ought always to give thanks to God for you, brethren, as is only fitting, because your faith is greatly enlarged, and the love of each one of you toward one another grows ever greater; therefore, we ourselves speak proudly of you among the churches of God for your perseverance and faith in the midst of all your persecutions and afflictions which you endure. (2 Thess. 1:3–4)

The famous novelist Victor Hugo stated, "Man lives more by affirmation than by bread."[5] Paul recognized that this struggling congregation needed affirmation and encouragement. The Thessalonian believers did not need criticism or pity. Rather, they needed sustenance for the hard journey. They needed an anchor to keep them steady as they were buffeted by the waves of persecution and the winds of heresy. From these two verses above, we observe two principles modeled by Paul.

Divine Perspective Gives Us the Impetus to Affirm Others

Paul could have simply sighed and said, "I'm so sorry," or "This, too, shall pass." Instead, Paul encouraged the Thessalonians to find meaning in faith-stretching trials and love-strengthening challenges.

5. Victor Hugo, as quoted by Lars Wilhelmsson in *Making Forever Friends* (Torrance, Calif.: the Martin Press, 1982), p. 66.

He knew that God never allows a test without a purpose. He demonstrated to the Thessalonian believers that divine perspective gave him the impetus to affirm others. He focused on their love for one another and pointed out that their faith was increasing. God was still working!

Two phrases in 2 Thessalonians 1:3–4 jump off the page: "we give thanks to God for you" and "we ourselves speak proudly of you." Paul exuberantly commended to God and man the enduring example of the Thessalonians.

Depth Perception Gives Us the Insight to Affirm Others

While divine perspective gives us the *motivation* to affirm others, depth perception provides us with the *insight* to affirm them. Paul recognized the love, *perseverance*, and faith of the Thessalonian believers. Note here that the word for perseverance means "to abide under."[6] Picture a lonely burro laden with packs, trudging over arid hills. His burden weighs heavily on his back, but he makes his way slowly and surely to his final destination. He "abides under" his load, just as the Thessalonians endured the pressure of their antagonistic culture.

Paul saw beyond this congregation's temporal situation. He knew that the endurance gained through trials would produce tried-and-true character. And he reminded these believers that only through pressure are grapes transformed into wine.

When we choose to affirm others, we affirm the positive character traits forming within them. Notice that Paul does not pray that the Thessalonians' affliction will diminish. Rather, he offers assurance and affirmation that their character had grown and flourished. God had answered the prayer Paul prayed in 1 Thessalonians 3:12:

> May the Lord cause you to increase and abound in
> love for one another, and for all people, just as we
> also do for you.

From Thessalonica to Your Town

Though our places of worship may be free from mob violence or deceitful heresies, we all experience affliction. Like Paul, we need

---

6. W. E. Vine, *Vine's Complete Expository Dictionary of Old and New Testament Words*, ed. W. E. Vine and F. F. Bruce, electronic ed. (Old Tappan, N.J.: Revell, 1981; Published in electronic form by Logos Research Systems, 1996), p. 30.

to respond quickly when those around us feel crushed under a personal winepress. Here are three applicable commands we can act on today.

Look Around

The great nineteenth-century preacher Joseph Parker stated, "In every pew there is a broken heart. Speak often on suffering and you will never lack for a congregation."[7] Our churches should be hospitals for hurting hearts. Take time to look beyond the polished veneer of those you encounter week to week. The tailored suits, expensive cars, carefully-manicured nails, and designer dresses cannot hide the hurting souls of the men and women around us. The writer of the book of Proverbs stated, "Even in laughter the heart may be in pain, and the end of joy may be grief" (Prov. 14:13). Ask the Father for discernment to see His children through His eyes.

Reach Out

Though preoccupied with various duties in Corinth, Paul wasted no time in addressing the doctrinal doubt expressed by the Thessalonians. But he delivered the truth with kid gloves. Paul not only cleared up the misunderstanding, he also expressed sympathy with their afflictions. The word *sympathy* comes from a Greek word meaning "to suffer together."[8] Our words carry more weight when we are willing to suffer alongside those who hurt.

Speak Up

Paul packs this chapter with personal affirmations: "we give thanks for you . . . we speak proudly of you . . . we pray for you always . . ." (2 Thess. 1:3, 4, 11). As wise Solomon exhorted, "Anxiety in a man's heart weighs it down, but a good word makes it glad" (Prov. 12:25). Take it upon yourself to speak a good word today and make someone's heart glad.

When your body aches, you intentionally seek to remedy the affliction. With the same fervor, we ought to *look around, reach out, and speak up* when those in the body of Christ experience pain.

7. Joseph Parker, *Leadership* magazine, as quoted by Charles R. Swindoll, *The Tale of the Tardy Oxcart and 1,501 Other Stories* (Nashville, Tenn.: Word Publishing, 1998), p. 459.

8. See Walter Bauer, F. Wilbur Gingrich, and Frederick W. Danker, *A Greek-English Lexicon of the New Testament and Other Early Christian Literature* (Chicago, Ill.: University of Chicago Press, 1979), p. 779; accessed through the Logos Library System.

Like the Thessalonians, you have the choice to relate well with others. Instead of shattering under pressure, allow yourself to be vulnerable and open. Let intimacy and love bring forth the "wine" of blessing in your life.

Living Insights

Find a pen and open your Bible to 2 Thessalonians. Read through the book and mark each passage containing the name "Lord Jesus Christ" or "Lord Jesus." You should find nine references to the full name of Christ and three other references to "the Lord Jesus." Paul took pains to assure the Thessalonians that even through their plight, Jesus was Lord. The majesty of Jesus beams through the fog of heretical challenges and government persecutions.

Have you experienced any struggles in the past that have caused a cloud of doubt to descend on your faith? If so, what were they?

_____

_____

_____

_____

_____

_____

How do you usually respond when struggles and difficult situations arise? To whom do you turn for guidance and encouragement in hard times?

_____

_____

_____

_____

Reflect on the words Jesus spoke in Matthew 6:25–34. Remember that Christ is King despite the chaos in our lives and that God's faithfulness endures to all generations. Trusting God through the tough times stretches the very fabric of our faith.

Let's face it—we're all starving for affirmation. Self-help books teach us how to raise our self-esteem. Mid-afternoon talk shows exhort us to "love ourselves." Our spouses wonder why the praises poured out lavishly in courtship dried up somewhere between our careers and our kids. We strive to gain recognition at work, at home, and even at church. Sometimes we worry so much about *receiving* affirmation and compliments that we fail to give them.

Think about the last time you received a meaningful compliment. What was it, and why did it touch your heart? Share your answer with the group.

Next, write down the name of someone you know who has persevered under pressure or whose faith is currently being tested.

Now, team up into groups of two or three and pray for each person listed. Then write down specific ways you can affirm these people this week. You might decide to write them letters, give them a phone call, or treat them to a dinner out. Be tangibly creative.

One day God will bestow upon us His *glory*. C. S. Lewis defined glory as "fame with God, approval or . . . 'appreciation' by God."[9] On that day God will lavish on us a "divine accolade."[10] Until then, something in us hungers for appreciation, honor, or a simple "Thank you." We long to hear the words "Well done, my good and faithful servant."

9. C. S. Lewis, *The Weight of Glory and Other Addresses* (San Francisco, Calif.: HarperSanFrancisco, HarperCollins, 2001), p. 36.

10. Lewis, *The Weight of Glory*, p. 36.

Chapter 2

WHEN GOD GETS THE LAST WORD

2 Thessalonians 1:5–10

This is the "now" generation. When pain comes, we want relief— now. When wrong occurs, we demand justice—now. When disease strikes, we expect healing—now.

From fast food to fast relief, we seek drive-through-window solutions to the wide range of painful experiences we encounter in life. Raised on thirty-second commercials and thirty-minute sit-coms, we want our life's problems to be packaged in small, neatly-wrapped boxes. But just when we think we've finally tied the bow around our struggles, our pain resurfaces and kicks out a side of the box. We sit amid the ruined cardboard and crumpled wrapping, disillusioned and despondent.

The book of 2 Thessalonians teaches us to think outside our "problem boxes." Paul empathized with our struggles, answered some hard questions, and provided perspective on the pain and suffering that we all inevitably endure.

A Statement of Our Struggle

In his book *When Bad Things Happen to Good People*, Rabbi Harold Kushner asked the question that rises in our minds like a dark, nebulous cloud:

> Why do bad things happen to good people? All other theological conversation is intellectually diverting; somewhat like doing the crossword puzzle in the Sunday paper and feeling very satisfied when you have made the words fit; but ultimately without the capacity to reach people where they really care.[1]

The problem of pain presents a major stumbling block to our understanding of God. Often, when believers suffer, we begin to

---

1. Harold S. Kushner, *When Bad Things Happen to Good People* (New York, N.Y.: Avon Books, 1983), p. 6.

doubt our Father's power and love. Suddenly overtaken by persecution or affliction, we find ourselves, like Jacob, wrestling in the dark with an overpowering force (see Gen. 32:24–26). We strive to know God, understand His will, and receive His blessing. But often He seems distant and alien to us, and we begin to wonder if He really cares.

In his book *The Problem of Pain*, C. S. Lewis masterfully addressed the issue of why bad things happen to good people. He articulated the faulty intellectual argument that many people make regarding the problem of pain:

> "If God were good, He would wish to make His creatures perfectly happy, and if God were almighty, He would be able to do what He wished. But the creatures are not happy. Therefore God lacks either goodness, or power, or both." This is the problem of pain, in its simplest form.[2]

Rabbi Kushner followed this basic argument in *When Bad Things Happen to Good People*. He recognized the goodness of God, but failed to realize that the Father also requires holiness and justice and that pain results from the effects of human sinfulness in the world, as a consequence of the Fall. Thus, Kushner wrongly concluded that bad things happen to good people because God lacks the power to prevent suffering.

In contrast, C. S. Lewis focused on God's sovereign purposes that are often revealed in the face of suffering. He noted that God's purpose is not as much to prevent suffering in this world as it is to sanctify people. Jesus prophesied in John 16:33: "These things I have spoken to you, so that in Me you may have peace. In the world you have tribulation, but take courage; I have overcome the world." God is both good and powerful, and He uses human pain and suffering to draw His children back to Him. C. S. Lewis noted:

> Pain insists upon being attended to. God whispers to us in our pleasures, speaks in our conscience, but shouts in our pains: it is His megaphone to rouse a deaf world.[3]

---

2. C. S. Lewis, *The Problem of Pain* (New York, N.Y.: Macmillan Co., 1970), p. 26.

3. Lewis, *The Problem of Pain*, p. 93.

Paul Addressed the Problem of Pain

In the book of 2 Thessalonians, Paul addressed the problem of pain by reminding believers that God uses suffering to accomplish His purposes in their lives. In verses 5–10 of chapter 1, Paul took a step back from the persecutions and afflictions experienced by the believers in Thessalonica to view the fragments of their pain in the broader context of a purposeful eternity. From that, a whole picture emerged, bathed in such a glorious light that it banished every shadow ever cast on the character of God. Much has been written concerning human pain and suffering, but we'll see that God gets the last word.

An Answer to Our Question

Through our tears, the image of God often becomes blurred. Our painful experiences cause us to perceive God as standing in some far-off corner of our lives—distant, indifferent, and powerless. We misinterpret His patience as absence, His deferment of judgment as a deplorable lack of justice. Romans 11:33 refocuses our understanding of God:

> Oh, the depth of the riches both of the wisdom and knowledge of God! How unsearchable are His judgments and unfathomable His ways!

What we label unjust and unfair, Paul called unsearchable and unfathomable. Since God doesn't set His time by our clock, we often find ourselves out of sync with His purposes. And since He doesn't take His cues from our script, we find ourselves caught up in a drama penned by another Hand (see Isa. 55:8–9). In the tragic scenes of our lives, we cry out for relief and restitution—now. When we don't get an immediate answer, we feel God either doesn't hear, doesn't care, or can't help.

The six verses we study in this lesson raise the curtain on the time when God, as the Playwright, will have the last word. Then we will find that our discordant experiences of pain were but the orchestra warming up for the most marvelous drama in the history of the universe—the return of Christ.

A Perspective on our Problem

As we studied the first portion of 2 Thessalonians 1, we noted that the Thessalonian church had been going through strenuous times of persecution and affliction. Having affirmed the people's faith and perseverance, Paul turned their thoughts toward the glorious kingdom of God:

> This is a plain indication[4] of God's righteous judgment so that you will be considered worthy of the kingdom of God, for which indeed you are suffering. (2 Thess. 1:5)

As we look at suffering from God's perspective, two observations come into view. First, whatever your circumstances, *your trials are not a result of some divine oversight.* To us, suffering seems to deny, rather than prove, that God is working out His righteous judgment. From our perspective, suffering is an evil to be avoided at all costs. But from the perspective of the New Testament, it is the character-building cost of following Christ.

Secondly, *suffering for Christ is an initiation into the kingdom of God.* In verse 5, Paul assures the Thessalonians that they are not experiencing God's judgment, but an entrance into the kingdom of God.

A Reprieve from Our Pain

While our present pain indicates an initiation, we are also promised a future vindication through God's righteous judgment. Second Thessalonians 1:6–7 reveals the two aspects of God's righteous judgment:

> For after all it is only just for God to repay with affliction those who afflict you, and to give relief to you who are afflicted and to us as well when the Lord Jesus will be revealed from heaven with His mighty angels in flaming fire.

When the Lord Jesus is revealed, He will both *repay* those who afflict and *relieve* those who are afflicted.[5] His coming will be the

---

4. Literally, "manifest token." On one side, suffering is a vivid token of God's presence, a reminder that we are pilgrims in a strange land, inhabitants of another kingdom. On the other side, the fact that the Thessalonians manifested endurance and faith in the midst of suffering was a token of the enduring kingdom to come, one whose King will issue a righteous judgment that will reward the afflicted and crush those who afflict. The meaning of *worthy* here is "to declare worthy" as opposed to "to make worthy." See Luke 7:7 for a similar sense.

5. The word *repay* conveys the idea of a payment in full for receipts due (see also Rom. 12:19). The word *relief* denotes a relaxing of tension as in the slackening of a taut bowstring.

most dramatic event of history. He will be literally unveiled from heaven "with His mighty angels in flaming fire." When Jesus returns as King of Kings, His purpose will be to administer "righteous judgment" (2 Thess. 1:5). His return will be glorious, but His justice will wield a sharp sword of separation:

> . . . dealing out retribution to those who do not know God and to those who do not obey the gospel of our Lord Jesus. These will pay the penalty of eternal destruction, away from the presence of the Lord and from the glory of His power. (vv. 8–9)

The Gospel is an invitation from the King of Kings and Lord of Lords. Its very offer is a royal compliment of the highest order. On the other hand, refusing the offer is the greatest insult. And no refusal will go unanswered. God will have the last word. Those to whom He says, "Depart from Me!" will be eternally banished from His presence (see Matt. 25:41).

In his sermon "The Weight of Glory," C. S. Lewis captured the horror of that moment:

> We are warned that it may happen to any one of us to appear at last before the face of God and hear only the appalling words: "I never knew you. Depart from Me." In some sense, as dark to the intellect as it is unendurable to the feelings, we can be both banished from the presence of Him who is present everywhere and erased from the knowledge of Him who knows all. We can be left utterly and absolutely outside—repelled, exiled, estranged, finally and unspeakably ignored.[6]

Such is the fate of those who refuse the royal invitation. However, extraordinary blessings await the believer, as C. S. Lewis also noted:

> On the other hand, we can be called in, welcomed, received, acknowledged. . . . Apparently, then, our lifelong nostalgia, our longing to be reunited with something in the universe from which we now

---

6. C. S. Lewis, *The Weight of Glory and Other Addresses* (Grand Rapids, Mich.: William B. Eerdmans Publishing Co., 1974), p. 12.

feel cut off, to be on the inside of some door which we have always seen from the outside, is no mere neurotic fancy, but the truest index of our real situation. And to be at last summoned inside would be both glory and honour beyond all our merits and also the healing of that old ache.[7]

A Concluding Application

If you're a believer, Christ's return will be your moment to shine—with the King! His glory will bring an end to all suffering (see Rom. 8:18). This will not be the closing curtain that ends your life's drama, but the curtain that unveils a whole new stage and begins a whole new play—one in which persecution and affliction have no part. Because you accepted the Gospel at a decisive moment in time, you can live with the sustaining hope and certainty that you will be included in the eternal event described in 2 Thessalonians 1:10. Take some time to meditate on that thought!

If you're not a believer when the Lord Jesus returns, all the glory you've amassed during your life will be like the ephemeral streak of a shooting star falling into the outer darkness, eternally away from His presence. The royal invitation of the Gospel has been sent R.S.V.P. Won't you accept this gracious offer so you can be in heaven to share in His glory? Unless you choose to believe in Jesus Christ, you will someday face the endless horrors of eternal hell at an infinite distance away from God (2 Thess. 1:9). Take some time to seriously consider this thought: The decision to receive Christ will be the most important decision you will ever make. Seek Him today while He may be found.

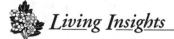 *Living Insights*

We serve a King whose kingdom is not of this world. The only crown He ever wore on earth was made of thorns. Jesus warned His disciples that if men persecuted Him, they would be persecuted also (see John 15:20). He told them, "'If the world hates you, you know that it has hated Me before it hated you'" (v. 18).

---

7. Lewis, *The Weight of Glory*, p. 12.

Recognize that you serve a King who, though He was raised, was first crucified. Therefore, don't think it unusual when you encounter fiery trials that test your faith (James 1:2–4; 1 Peter 4:12). As George Macdonald once wrote: "The Son of God suffered unto the death, not that men might not suffer, but that their sufferings might be like His."[8] Realizing this, we can rejoice to be counted worthy to suffer for His name (Acts 5:41).

When you carry the load of your suffering to the Lord in prayer, do you ask for lighter burdens or a stronger back? How can you change the way you pray in light of this study?

How often do you approach God with resentment over trials and burdens? How can you make rejoicing and thanksgiving a more vital part of your spiritual life?

Digging Deeper

God will enact His righteous judgment when Jesus Christ returns. Unbelievers will experience eternal doom, while believers will enter God's presence in heaven. Heaven will be a glorious place! Some believers may ask, "But won't heaven's joy be tainted by our awareness that our unsaved loved ones are in hell?"[9] It's a tough question. You may have had an unbelieving spouse, sibling, parent, or friend whom you loved dearly and who passed away without knowing Christ. If so, this issue weighs heavily on your heart.

Bible scholar J. I. Packer noted in "Hell's Final Enigma" that there

8. George Macdonald, as quoted by C. S. Lewis in *The Problem of Pain*, epigraph.

9. See J. I. Packer, "Good Question: Hell's Final Enigma," *Christianity Today*, April 22, 2002, p. 84

are no grounds for believing that our memory of these people will be erased in heaven. We will be aware of their circumstances. So how could this fact *not* keep us from experiencing the total joy of heaven?

Scripture tells us that God the Father now pleads with men and women to accept the reconciliation and forgiveness that Christ's death secured for us. Jesus loves all of humanity dearly, but He will express the wrath of God and administer justice as a righteous judge. God's holiness and perfection will be revealed as the Father vindicates Himself against sin (see Matt. 25; John 5:22–29; Rom. 2:5–16; 12:19; 2 Thess. 1:7–9). And *all* those who are aligned with Him—angels, saints, and martyrs—will praise Him for His righteousness. We will approve the judgment of sin, even if that means the judgment of those we have known and loved.

How can this be? Packer noted:

> Remember, in heaven our minds, hearts, motives, and feelings will be sanctified, so that we are fully conformed to the character and outlook of Jesus our Lord. This will happen at or before our bodily resurrection. How we shall then think and feel is really beyond our knowing, just as a chrysalis could not know what it feels like to be a butterfly until it becomes one.[10]

God promises in Revelation 7:17 that He will wipe away every tear from the eyes of believers. In heaven, glorifying our Father and praising Him will occupy all of our time. We will be transformed! Our love and joy will no longer be overshadowed by any pain or grief; pity for hell's occupants will not enter our hearts.

Packer added, "Granted, this sounds to us more like hard-heartedness than Christlikeness, yet Christlikeness is precisely what it will be."[11] While we cannot conceive of this heavenly condition in our present state, we will one day be like Christ. As Paul wrote in 1 Corinthians 13:12, "For now we see in a mirror dimly, but then face to face; now I know in part, but then I will know fully just as I also have been fully known." Our hope for the future is grounded in the knowledge of our God. We're responsible to share the truth of the Gospel with our loved ones while we have the chance.

10. Packer, "Hell's Final Enigma," p. 84.
11. Packer, "Hell's Final Enigma," p. 84.

 *Small Group Insights*

The streets of New York, Chicago, and Los Angeles teem with disheveled men and women draped with placards reading: "Repent, the end is near!" or "Judgment cometh! Are you ready?" We give them about as much thought as Chicken Little received when he ran to and fro squawking, "The sky is falling! The sky is falling!" In our fast-paced society, the "here and now" is so urgent that it's hard to focus on the future.

Because we, as believers, have a guaranteed inheritance in heaven, God's judgment often does not seem relevant. However, God will act as righteous judge and jury to us as well as to those who do not know Him. For evidence, take the time now to read Hebrews 9:27–28, 2 Peter 3:7, and John 5:19–24.

How will believers be judged?

_____

_____

_____

How will nonbelievers be judged?

_____

_____

_____

In light of this knowledge, how can we live with the end in mind?

_____

_____

_____

Read 1 Thessalonians 5:1–11. How can we as Christians be "alert and sober" in this age?

_____

_____

_____

Chapter 3

PRAYING FOR OTHERS: A MUST

2 Thessalonians 1:11–12

It had to be tough. While the apostle Paul was earnestly preaching in Corinth (see Acts 18:1–5), his dear Christian friends in Thessalonica were going through the wringer of persecution. How he must have wished he could do something, anything, to help these believers he loved so much.

It's tough to be somewhere else when those we care about are suffering, isn't it? Even when we're there, we often feel powerless to help. And somewhat apologetically, we say, "I'll pray for you," feeling that somehow it's not enough, like it's our last resort.

But nothing could be further from the truth.

A. J. Gordon reminds us, "You can never do more than pray until you have prayed."[1] Prayer is our first priority and our most powerful means of helping. Why? Because in praying, we actively participate in what God is doing to bring about His will in the situation. We're co-laborers with God!

Paul recognized what a gift prayer is, and he modeled for us not only how to intercede for others but also how to give them new strength in the Lord so that His will is done.

Prayer: An Invaluable Discipline

To fully appreciate this privilege God has given us, let's get a handle on all that prayer is and what it does.

What Is Prayer?

Prayer is making deliberate contact with God in word or thought. It is the voice of faith, whose whisper can be felt across the street or across the world. It is what pries us from our seats as spectators and places us as active participants with God. Prayer expresses itself in many ways:

- an outpouring of praise

---

1. A. J. Gordon, as quoted by Ben Patterson in *Deepening Your Conversation with God* (Minneapolis, Minn.: Bethany House Publishers, 1999), p. 20.

- a confession of wrong

- a request for help

- a declaration of need

- a statement of thanks

- intercession for others

Through prayer, we draw near to God with confidence (Heb. 4:16); ask, seek, and knock at the door of His generosity (Matt. 7:7–8); release anxiety (Phil. 4:6–7); and gain wisdom (James 1:5). Prayer is the discipline of mind that is *always* appropriate for our needs (Eph. 6:18). And it is the way we align ourselves with the Lord to see as He sees and want what He wants.

Prayer is, in fact, such an invaluable discipline that we are urged to "pray without ceasing" (1 Thess. 5:17). This doesn't mean non-stop verbal praying—it means an attitude of prayer. As one student of Scripture has put it, "It means rather to live with Christ in such a way that you can talk with Him, or listen to Him at any moment."[2] There should be nothing between your soul and the Savior. Praying without ceasing is consciously living each moment in the presence of Christ.

Why Is Prayer Important?

First, prayer is important because it refocuses our perspective. Without prayer, we see only the visible; with prayer, God shows us the hidden dimensions of life. Second, it quiets our fears and calms our nerves. We may come to prayer fearful and anxious, but when we give our worries to the Lord, we come away calmed and assured (Phil. 4:6–7). Third, prayer transfers our burdens. It takes the big load we've been carrying and shifts it to the shoulders that can handle its weight (Matt. 11:28–29; 1 Pet. 5:7). Fourth, prayer upholds others who are in need. It is the way we help bear one another's burdens and lift them to the One who knows best.

Colossians 4:12 introduces us to a model intercessor:

> Epaphras, who is one of your number, a bondslave of
> Jesus Christ, sends you his greetings, *always laboring*

---

2. Donald Grey Barnhouse, *Thessalonians: An Expositional Commentary* (Grand Rapids, Mich.: Zondervan Publishing House, 1977), p. 82.

earnestly for you in his prayers, that you may stand perfect and fully assured in all the will of God. (emphasis added)

Intercession occurs when we "labor earnestly"[3] in prayer for others, emotionally and spiritually bearing their burdens and carrying them to the Lord. Paul does this and more in his prayer for the Thessalonians.

Prayer for Others: An Essential Involvement

So far in his letter, Paul had expressed thanksgiving for the Thessalonians' growing faith and love (2 Thess. 1:3), affirmed them for their perseverance in the midst of persecution (v. 4), reassured them of God's justice (vv. 5–9), and encouraged them in the hope of the Lord's coming (v. 10). In the next passage, he interceded for them:

> To this end also we pray for you always, that our God will count you worthy of your calling, and fulfill every desire for goodness and the work of faith with power, so that the name of our Lord Jesus will be glorified in you, and you in Him, according to the grace of our God and the Lord Jesus Christ. (2 Thess. 1:11–12)

Note the constancy of Paul's prayer—his heart was "always" occupied with these believers, wanting three things for them in the light of the Lord's glorious return: (1) that God would count them worthy of their calling; (2) that He would fulfill their desire for goodness and the work of faith with power; and (3) that the name of Jesus Christ would be glorified in them.

Worthy of Their Calling

Paul's first request is reminiscent of verse 5: "that you will be considered worthy of the kingdom of God." Instead of asking that God might remove the hardship and stop the persecution, Paul

---

3. The Greek word is *agonizomai* from *agon* which means "contest, struggle." These words were often used in relation to the stadium and took on the figurative meaning of contending and striving—seeing "life as a struggle with a prize." Gerhard Kittel and Gerhard Friedrich, eds., *Theological Dictionary of the New Testament*, translated and abridged in one volume by Geoffrey W. Bromiley (1985; reprint, Grand Rapids, Mich.: William B. Eerdmans Publishing Co., 1992), pp. 20–21.

asked that the suffering believers might live up to their high calling, which was "not only to believe in Him, but also to suffer for His sake" (Phil. 1:29).

When faced with pain or difficulty, our usual inclination is to toss up a rescue prayer. We ask God to make the hurt stop. We beg Him for relief from the pressure and strain. Yet Paul does not ask the Lord to take away the Thessalonians' affliction. It's not that he didn't care for them—he did very much. But Paul wanted these persecuted believers to grow in their kingdom perspective. He wanted them to stay focused on the eternal glory God had in store for them and "to lead lives in keeping with their destiny."[4]

Goodness and Faith Fulfilled

In Paul's second request, he prayed that the Lord would bring to pass the Thessalonians' intentions to do good. Essentially, he addressed their attitude in the midst of their suffering. The word *goodness* (*agathosyne* in Greek) points to "moral excellence" and is listed among the fruits of the Spirit and of the Light (see Gal. 5:22; Eph. 5:9).[5] When suffering strikes, it's easy to want to strike back or give up on God's way. Paul's words to the Galatians encourage us: "Let us not lose heart in doing good, for in due time we will reap if we do not grow weary" (Gal. 6:9). The Thessalonians longed to emerge from their siege of suffering full of goodness, with their trust in God and their kindheartedness firmly intact. Paul prayed that their hopes would be fulfilled.

Paul then prayed for the Thessalonians' "work of faith," wanting their faith to reach fruition in a harvest of good works (see Eph. 2:10; 1 Thess. 1:3). The testimony of the Thessalonian believers had spread throughout the region (1 Thess. 1:7–8), yet they were plunged into difficulty. However, in the midst of affliction, they wanted to be known as people who walked by faith.

So Paul prayed along these lines, asking the Lord, who had inspired the Thessalonians toward faith and good works, to accomplish their desires with His own power. Simply put, he asked "that God [would] enable his people to demonstrate the reality of their

---

4. Thomas L. Constable, "2 Thessalonians," in *The Bible Knowledge Commentary*, New Testament edition, ed. John F. Walvoord and Roy B. Zuck (Colorado Springs, Colo.: Scripture Press Publications, Victor Books, 1983), p. 716.

5. Kittel and Friedrich, *Theological Dictionary of the New Testament*, p. 4.

faith in action."[6] Again, note that Paul didn't ask for the testing to cease or for relief from the pressure. Here we have another example of the truth that God's thoughts are not our thoughts and His ways are not our ways (see Isa. 55:8). We want relief; God wants deepening of character. We want out; God wants to see us through. We want to say it's over; God wants to say that the testing did its full work.

The purpose of all this can be seen in Paul's third request.

Jesus Christ Glorified

Paul wanted the Thessalonians to fully live out their faith in the midst of their suffering so "that the name of our Lord Jesus [would be] glorified in [them]" (2 Thess. 1:12a). The word *name* in Scripture's language "stands for the person named, his character, conduct, reputation, and everything else about him."[7] Christ's reputation is directly impacted by how we, as believers, live—we either exalt Him or we make a mockery of Him through our choices and conduct.

By humbling Himself to filter His glory through us, God gives the highest dignity not only to us but to our suffering. And by His grace, He glorifies us through Christ (v. 12b)! As the moon reflects the glory of the sun, without light of its own, so will we someday share the glory of Christ and be set in the heavens as a testimony to His beauty and faithfulness.

Enhancing Your Intercessory Prayer

Real joy comes in seeing our prayers align with God's work in the world. To help us move out of the realm of spectator and into being active participants in the things of God, here are some suggestions on how to pray more perceptively and purposefully.

- *Be specific.* Specific prayers are answered in specific ways. A brief glance at the rest of Paul's letter reveals how specifically he prayed. He prayed that the Thessalonians would be comforted and have their hearts strengthened (2 Thess. 2:17) and that they would have peace in every circumstance (3:16).

- *Read God's kingdom into the situations of others.* Look at what

---

6. I. Howard Marshall, "2 Thessalonians," in *New Bible Commentary: 21st Century Edition*, 4th ed., rev., ed. D. A. Carson and others (Downers Grove, Ill.: InterVarsity Press, 1994), p. 1288.

7. Constable, "2 Thessalonians," p. 717.

others are experiencing through kingdom eyes. And remember, suffering is a part of kingdom life. By understanding this, you'll not only have empathy but depth of perception as well.

- *Reflect on the development of other people's faith.* Reflect on the person's faith as much as you do on his or her pain. This will give you peace you otherwise wouldn't have had.

- *Remember the ultimate goal.* For the believer, the ultimate goal in life is to glorify God. Keeping this in mind will give you objectivity. Effective intercessory prayer is not necessarily praying for relief for the afflicted or even for removal of the affliction. It is praying purposefully in light of a kingdom perspective. It is praying with an understanding that there is a purpose to another's pain.

> It is easy to forget that at the heart of Christianity is a crucified God. God does not watch his suffering world with detachment. He comes into people's pain; agonizes and bleeds with them. This is the way he has chosen to repair the damage by working patiently and painfully inside the problem. . . .
>
> Even for Jesus there were some things that could only be learned through suffering. Paul discovered that God's grace was enough for him only through being tormented by a thorn in the flesh. Christians are called to believe, sometimes in the teeth of the evidence, that God can transform every situation.[8]

Won't you join the Lord in His work of meeting people in their pain and bringing them encouragement and healing? You're just an intercessory prayer away.

 *Living Insights*

Did you know that the Bible is brimming with prayers? It contains within its pages prayers of kings, psalmists, prophets, apostles, and the Lord Jesus Himself, as well as the prayers of ordinary people

---

8. David V. Day, "Suffering," in *The Bible for Everyday Life,* ed. George Carey and Robin Keeley (Grand Rapids, Mich.: William B. Eerdmans Publishing Co. by special arrangement with Lion Publishing, Oxford, England, 1996), pp. 385–86.

like us. Every intercessory prayer in the Scriptures is a prayer for specific people in specific circumstances with specific needs. So how do we apply these prayers to our own situations? In other words, how do we "pray the Scriptures"?

As we study God's Word, our thinking begins to be shaped by God's thoughts. Paul calls this "the renewing of your mind" (see Rom. 12:1–2). When we base our prayers on Scripture, we begin to see something of God's will for the person or situation for which we pray. Let's take some time to learn how to pray the Scriptures by using Paul's prayer in 2 Thessalonians 1:11–12 as an example.

Paul prayed for the believers in Thessalonica who were facing affliction and persecution. Is God bringing to your mind someone who is facing some kind of difficulty or challenge? Perhaps a son or daughter away at college, a missionary, a parent who is losing some abilities, a friend in the military, or someone for whom you are concerned? Jot down the names that come to mind.

_____

_____

_____

Now pray for these people by following Paul's pattern for prayer. Utilizing his three specific requests listed below, put his petitions in your own words. If you need to, refer to the concluding section in this chapter, "Enhancing Your Intercessory Prayer."

1. "That our God will count you worthy of your calling" (2 Thess. 1:11a):

_____

_____

_____

2. That He will "fulfill every desire for goodness and the work of faith with power" (v. 11b):

_____

_____

_____

3. That "the name of our Lord Jesus will be glorified in you, and you in Him" (v. 12):

_____

_____

_____

Once you have put the biblical prayer into your own words, spread your list of requests before the Lord as Hezekiah did (see 2 Kings 19:14) and pray as the Lord leads you. Commit yourself to praying for these people on a daily basis.

Small Group Insights

Professor M. Robert Mulholland Jr., in his book *Invitation to a Journey*, shares these insights into what prayer often becomes:

> We tend to think of prayer as something we *do* in order to produce the results we believe are needed or, rather, to get God to produce the results. Go into any Christian bookstore and note the number of books devoted to techniques of prayer. We are interested in knowing what works and developing the skills that will ensure that our prayers are effective. As a result, our prayer tends to be a shopping list of things to be accomplished, an attempt to manipulate the symptoms of our lives without really entering into a deep, vital, transforming relationship with God in the midst of what we think we need.[9]

Ouch. Does that hit uncomfortably close to home for you? How would you describe your current experience of prayer? Is it more like bringing God your shopping list or nurturing your relationship with Him?

_____

_____

9. M. Robert Mulholland Jr., *Invitation to a Journey: A Road Map for Spiritual Formation* (Downers Grove, Ill.: InterVarsity Press, 1993), p. 105.

Based on what you've learned in the lesson, what purpose do you think prayer serves? Is there a particular aspect of what it is or does that speaks to your heart?

_____

_____

When you pray for others, do you see beyond their immediate physical or emotional needs to their deeper spiritual needs, like Paul did with the Thessalonians? How important is this? Why? And why do we so easily forget about it?

_____

_____

Take time to read aloud 2 Thessalonians 1:12. How can the Lord's glory become more of a focus in your prayers? In your life?

_____

_____

Robert Mulholland gives us this definition of prayer:

> Prayer is the act by which the people of God become incorporated into the presence and action of God in the world. Prayer becomes a sacrificial offering of ourselves to God, to become agents of God's presence and action in the daily events and situations of our lives.[10]

As you gather together in prayer, rather than bringing another shopping list to the Lord, ask Him how He would like you to become an agent of His presence in your part of His world. Ask Him to transform and revitalize your prayer life, aligning your focus more with His will and His glory. And thank Him for wanting so much more for us than we want for ourselves.

10. Mulholland, _Invitation to a Journey_, p. 108.

Chapter 4

LAWLESSNESS: THE MAN AND THE MYSTERY
2 Thessalonians 2:1–12

Earthquakes. Books have been written about them, films have been made about them, but nothing can quite describe the unsettling terror of actually experiencing one.

In jolting shock waves that can split concrete in an instant, the earth rocks beneath your feet. Your legs wobble like a newborn colt's as you take tentative steps to steady yourself. All sense of balance and equilibrium are lost as you find yourself adrift on a sea of swaying steel. To make matters worse, after the main quake, you may experience aftershocks for days or weeks to follow, further undermining your shaky sense of security. From Alaska to Mexico and from China to Southern California, earthquakes devastate and stun entire communities and countries.

What earthquakes are to the regions they affect, the divine judgment of the Day of the Lord will be to the whole world. Every person on earth during that time will experience its tremors and destruction.

Paul had taught the Thessalonian believers about the Day of the Lord and its terrors. But apparently the church members had become confused about the timing, fearing that the quaking of God's judgment had already begun. The focus of our passage deals with Paul's attempt to steady the doctrinal legs of the church. Before we launch into his explanation, however, it might be helpful to back up a few steps and examine a few end-time terms.

Defining the Day of the Lord

Bible teacher Thomas Constable offers this definition of the *Day of the Lord*:

> The Day of the Lord is the period of history mentioned repeatedly in the Old Testament during which God will bring judgment and blessing on the people of the earth in a more direct, dramatic, and drastic way than ever before (compare Isa. 13:6, 9; Zeph. 1:14–16). From other New Testament revelation

28

concerning this period of time it is believed that this will begin after the Rapture of the church, and will include the Tribulation and the Millennium.[1]

Constable gives three terms that bear a closer look: *rapture, tribulation,* and *millennium.* Previously, in 1 Thessalonians, Paul had given detailed instruction about the Rapture of the church. The Rapture is that marvelous day when believers all over the world, living and dead, will be taken from earth to heaven in the twinkling of an eye to meet the Lord in the air (see 1 Thess. 4:13–18).

Paul intended his teaching on the Rapture to be a source of comfort for his readers and took special pains to make sure this event was not confused with the judgment of the Day of the Lord, which he describes in 1 Thessalonians 5:

> Now as to the times and the epochs, brethren, you have no need of anything to be written to you. For you yourselves know full well that the Day of the Lord will come just like a thief in the night. While they are saying, "Peace and safety!" then destruction will come upon them suddenly like labor pains upon a woman with child, and they will not escape. But you, brethren, are not in darkness, that the day would overtake you like a thief; for you are all sons of light and sons of day. We are not of night nor of darkness; so then let us not sleep as others do, but let us be alert and sober. (vv. 1–6)

Paul warned that the Day of the Lord will come suddenly. It will entail the Tribulation and the Millennium. The period of destruction known as the Tribulation[2] was foretold by the prophet Daniel (see Dan. 9:24–27) and described by Jesus (Matt. 24:7–9).

---

1. Thomas L. Constable, "2 Thessalonians," in *The Bible Knowledge Commentary,* New Testament edition, ed. John F. Walvoord and Roy B. Zuck (Wheaton, Ill.: Scripture Press Publication, Victor Books, 1983), p. 717. The term *Day of the Lord* occurs in the following passages: Isaiah 13:6, 9; Ezekiel 13:5; 30:3; Joel 1:15; 2:1, 11, 31, 3:14; Amos 5:18, 20; Obadiah 15; Zephaniah 1:7, 14; Malachi 4:5; Acts 2:20; 1 Thessalonians 5:2; 2 Thessalonians 2:2; 2 Peter 3:10. In addition, the phrases *that day, the day,* and *the great day* occur more than seventy-five times in the Old Testament.

2. Because the *Tribulation* is the worldwide outpouring of God's wrath and because "God has not destined [believers] for wrath" (1 Thess. 5:9), we can conclude that we will not go through the Tribulation. In the same way that Lot was taken out of Sodom before the outpouring of God's wrath, so we will be taken out of the world before the Tribulation.

According to Jesus, the shock wave of disasters will intensify to the point of almost total devastation (see Matt. 24:21–22a).

The Tribulation is merely Act 1 of the Day-of-the-Lord drama that will culminate with Christ's return in power (see Joel 3:12–17; Zeph. 1:14–18; and Rev. 6:12–17; 19). Having vanquished His foes, Christ will establish the millennial kingdom—His thousand-year reign on earth during which God will fulfill the promises that He made to David (see 2 Sam. 7:16; Ps. 89:3–4; 33–37; Rev. 20).

We can visualize the progression of these end-time events in a timeline like this:

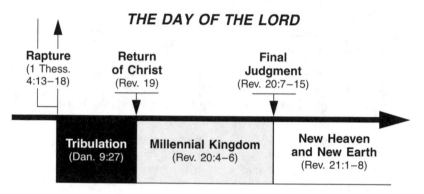

News of the confusion among the Thessalonian believers regarding the Day of the Lord immediately set Paul to work writing his second letter. As you recall, Paul spent the first chapter of 2 Thessalonians affirming and encouraging the believers who were experiencing persecution and affliction. In the next section, he directly addressed their confusion in order to ease the pounding of their fearful hearts.

Calming the Thessalonians' Fears

In Chapter 2, Paul clarified his teaching about the Rapture.

Clarifying the Coming of Christ

Paul began with Christ's "gathering together" of the Christians at the beginning of the Day of the Lord.

> Now we request you, brethren, with regard to the coming of our Lord Jesus Christ and our gathering together to Him, that you not be quickly shaken

from your composure or be disturbed either by a spirit or a message or a letter as if from us, to the effect that the Day of the Lord has come. (vv. 1–2)[3]

The Day of the Lord won't come until Jesus Christ sweeps His followers from the earth and gathers them together with Him in the sky. The rumor had spread, however, based on a "spirit or a message or a letter" supposedly from Paul, that the Day of the Lord had begun. The implication was that Christ had come for the church without taking the Thessalonian believers with Him. What a terrifying thought! Other Thessalonians speculated that maybe Paul had changed his teaching, that the Day of the Lord would come first—before the Rapture. Either way, they were confused and panicky.

With calming words, Paul corrected the false report by reviewing the order of end-time events and explaining how to recognize the Day of the Lord.

Explaining the Day of the Lord

Four words summarize Paul's description of the Day of the Lord: *defiance*, *delay*, *destruction*, and *delusion*. His point was that the Day of the Lord couldn't have begun because these warning signs had yet to appear.

The Defiance

In verses 3 and 4, Paul outlined a chronology of events that will mark the first stages of the Day of the Lord:

> Let no one in any way deceive you, for it will not come unless the apostasy comes first, and the man of lawlessness is revealed, the son of destruction, who opposes and exalts himself above every so-called god or object of worship, so that he takes his seat in the temple of God, displaying himself as being God. (2 Thess. 2:3–4)

---

3. The verb translated *gathering together* may have been something of a technical term. The verb form is also found in Matthew 24:31 and Mark 13:27. The noun form occurs again in Hebrews 10:25, translated as "assembling together." The verb *shaken* in the original language points to a sudden action rather than a continuous one. It's a verb that is often used to mean a literal shaking, especially of a violent nature, as produced by a wind, wave, or earthquake. The verb *disturbed*, however, is in the present tense and denotes a continuing state of worry and fear, as might be caused by continuing aftershocks.

At the onset of the Day of the Lord, a widespread apostasy, or renunciation of religious faith,[4] will take place such as has never occurred.[5] Then the "man of lawlessness" will be revealed. A man of enormous charisma, he will emerge through the din of Tribulation chaos and sweep the world's population off its feet with his pragmatic answers and vision for a united government. He will be persuasive, politically sophisticated, and marvelously convincing, performing miracles, signs, and wonders—so much so that the world will hail him as their leader and worship him as deity.

Who is this Satan-empowered man of lawlessness? The apostle John wrote of various antichrists who actively opposed Christianity during his day (1 John 4:3). But John also used the word *antichrist* as a proper noun for one person who is the absolute embodiment of evil (2:18). People who have stood watch over the prophetic horizon throughout the centuries have tried to identify this man. Their guesses crop up in every century, from a first-century Nero to a twentieth-century Hitler.[6]

This man is yet to be revealed and won't be until the dark age of apostasy engulfs the world, so Paul assured the Thessalonians that they could be confident that the Day of the Lord hadn't begun.

The Delay

Verses 5–7 form a parenthesis to Paul's discussion. Here, he noted the reason for the delay of this man entering the political spotlight:

> Do you not remember that while I was still with you, I was telling you these things? And you know what restrains him now, so that in his time he will be revealed. For the mystery of lawlessness is already at work; only he who now restrains will do so until he is taken out of the way. (2 Thess. 2:5–7)

The main mystery to us in this passage is the definition of the

---

4. *Merriam-Webster's Collegiate Dictionary*, 10th ed., see "apostasy."

5. The definite article with the word *apostasy* indicates a specific time of revolt against the things of God. Great turning points in history are noted by the placement of a definite article: *the* Dark Ages, *the* Reformation, *the* Renaissance. The turning point that will usher in the Day of the Lord will be "*the* Apostasy." The word *apostasy* literally means "falling away" but is also used to describe political and military rebellions.

6. For a more complete discussion, see Leon Morris, *The First and Second Epistles to the Thessalonians*, rev. ed., The New International Commentary on the New Testament series (Grand Rapids, Mich.: William B. Eerdmans Publishing Co., 1991), pp. 220–21.

"restraining influence" mentioned in verses 6–7. Some have proposed that the restraining influence of government is in view, but the use of the personal pronoun *he* in verse 7 suggests otherwise.

The restraining influence may also be the Holy Spirit. The Holy Spirit restrained wicked humankind during the days of Noah, when the Lord said, "My Spirit shall not strive with man forever" (Genesis 6:3). When man's wickedness exhausted God's long-suffering mercy, God's wrath spilled over the earth in judgment. According to Matthew 24:37–39, the situation of the end times parallels the days of Noah, so perhaps Paul had the Spirit of God in mind as the restraining influence here as well.

Today, the Holy Spirit restrains the world's lawlessness chiefly through the church. His presence in believers shines as the light of the world and permeates secular culture as the salt of the earth (Matt. 5:13–16). When the church is taken to be with Christ in the air, the light will be extinguished, and the salt will be removed. In the resulting darkness, every vestige of goodness will evaporate; every remnant of truth will unravel. It is at that time when the man of lawlessness will take center stage. Like animals bolting from cages in a zoo suddenly opened, lawlessness will run rampant through the streets when the restraining influence is taken out of the way.

Ours is a day of grace in which sin, to a large degree, is restrained. However, a time will come when God will deal definitively with sin. And that will be a time of great destruction.

The Destruction

Verses 8–10 of 2 Thessalonians recount the final match of Christ versus Antichrist when Jesus will return in power (see also Rev. 19):

> Then that lawless one will be revealed whom the Lord will slay with the breath of His mouth and bring to an end by the appearance of His coming; that is, the one whose coming is in accord with the activity of Satan, with all power and signs and false wonders, and with all the deception of wickedness for those who perish, because they did not receive the love of the truth so as to be saved. (2 Thess. 2:8–10)

With a mere breath from the Lord's mouth, the contest will be over. In the beginning, God spoke worlds into existence out of nothing; similarly, during the end times, God will merely breathe and His archenemy will be cast into oblivion.

The Delusion

Before the man of lawlessness is defeated, many will believe in him, primarily because of the power, signs, and wonders that will be manifested through him.[7] These people will reject the truth and instead cling to a delusion. God's response to this is seen in the final verses of our study.

> For this reason God will send upon them a deluding influence so that they will believe what is false, in order that they all may be judged who did not believe the truth, but took pleasure in wickedness. (2 Thess. 2:11–12)

If you compare this passage with Romans 1:18–32, you will see the same judicial principle at work — *light rejected brings certain darkness.* Spiritual and moral darkness will shroud the earth during the man of lawlessness' reign. But a day will dawn during that dark age when the Light of the World will return. Tyranny will be dethroned, darkness dispelled . . . and the glory of the Lord will bathe the earth in goodness, beauty, and truth.

An End-Times Application

What do these verses about the end times and the coming of Christ stir within you? Does your heart give a sigh of relief to know that Christ will guard you from God's future judgment of the world? If so, turn that relief and gratitude into a brief prayer of thanksgiving to the Lord as you anticipate the joy of meeting Him in the air someday.

Or does the image of coming disaster strike fear into your soul because the Day of the Lord may signal your day of reckoning and you're not prepared to face God? What the apostle Paul wrote to comfort his readers may disturb you . . . or it may have set you thinking about friends or family members who aren't prepared to stand before their Judge. In the Living Insights section, we'll look at the one way God has given us to be certain that our destiny is safe with Him. You don't want to miss this . . . read on!

---

7. The terms *power, signs,* and *wonders* are all used of the miracles of Christ. As closely as he can, the Antichrist will counterfeit the works of Christ as he declares himself to be the world's Messiah.

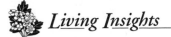

Living Insights

What's the most important item that you carry with you when you travel overseas? Your wallet? Your credit cards? Your plane ticket? All of these are crucial, but any seasoned traveler will tell you that the one item you can't afford to be without is your passport.

It's odd to think that a little booklet containing your picture and personal information is so vital. Why? Because this document is the official record of who you are and where you belong, your identity and your citizenship. Passport in hand, you can proceed unhindered through your country's customs gate to the sound of those wonderful words we all long to hear when traveling: *Welcome home!*

Wouldn't you like to own a passport to heaven? One that gives you complete confidence that someday you can walk straight through the celestial gates to your home with God? You can have such a passport—not in paper form, but in the form of a Person. The apostle John tells us His name:

> And the testimony is this, that God has given us eternal life, and this life is in His Son. He who has the Son has the life; he who does not have the Son of God does not have the life.
>
> These things I have written to you who believe in the name of the Son of God, so that you may know that you have eternal life. (1 John 5:11–13)

Faith is the only requirement to receive Jesus Christ, and once you have received Him, you have God's promise of eternal life. Your relationship with Jesus Christ is your divine passport that proclaims who you are—a child of God—and where you belong—in heaven (see 1 John 3:1–2; Phil. 3:20).

If you've never put your faith in Christ as your Savior, and you would like to now, here's a simple prayer you can use to express your desire:

> Dear God,
> I know that my sin has put a barrier between us. Thank You for sending Jesus to die in my place. I accept Your gift of eternal life and ask Jesus to be my Savior. Please begin to guide my life. In Jesus' name, Amen.

35

Perhaps you've trusted Christ as your Savior already, but you're concerned about friends or loved ones who will one day face their eternity without the Savior. Won't you make a commitment to tell them about Jesus? Maybe the passport illustration will help you express to them their need of Christ. Everyone wants to hear these reassuring words when they come to the gates of heaven: *Welcome home!*

Small Group Insights

Read Matthew 13:24–30 as a group. The disciples, confused about the meaning of this parable, asked Jesus for an explanation. His reply is found in 13:37–43:

> "The one who sows the good seed is the Son of Man
> . . . and the tares are the sons of the evil one. . . .
> The Son of Man will send forth His angels, and they
> will gather . . . those who commit lawlessness, and
> will throw them into the furnace. . . . Then the
> righteous will shine forth as the sun."

How will Christ's return be similar to a harvest? How will the righteous be rewarded?

_____

_____

_____

What have you learned about the Day of the Lord from this chapter? How will God judge those who reject Him?

_____

_____

_____

How does your knowledge of end-time events affect your ministry to others?

_____

_____

_____

Chapter 5

LIGHT FOR DARK DAYS

2 Thessalonians 2:13–17

Approximately one out of every 400,000 babies is born with a rare genetic disease known as *familial dysautonomia*. This disease prevents a child from feeling pain. At first reflection, the inability to experience pain may seem like a blessing. Imagine the possibilities— a football player who doesn't feel the pain of contact; a boxer who can endure a terrible beating in the ring and not feel the hurt; a woman who can bear children without the pain of childbirth.

The tragedy is that a child with this disease will never live long enough to know the glory of the gridiron or the joy of childbirth. Such a child will receive cuts, burns, and broken bones—never feeling anything. A cavity will rot the tooth without an ache. A broken bone will puncture the skin before anyone is aware of the fracture. An appendix will burst without a sharp pain in the side.

So, in some ways, pain *can* be good. It can be God's warning device that something is wrong—like a red light on the dashboard that alerts you to the fact that the engine is hot or the battery is low or the oil pressure is dropping. Pain can also be a signal of something very, very right that's just in transition. Whether from youthful muscles exerted in play or from a birth canal stretched to seemingly impossible limits, pain signals change, growth, development—the birth of something new.

There are many kinds of pain—physical, emotional, spiritual— each with its own kind of intensity. Pain can be a chronic, dull discomfort, or it can be a sudden jolt of such magnitude that it causes you to reel and collapse. Pain often seems pointless, but God assures us that it is always purposeful (Rom. 8:28).

Five Reasons We Suffer

Pain is a part of life. In God's curriculum, it is a course we can neither drop nor simply audit. But in seeing the course through to semester's end, we receive full credit on our final transcript—"the eternal weight of glory" (see 2 Cor. 4:16–18). At the beginning of a semester, course objectives are outlined in each professor's syllabus. Similarly, with regard to pain, God has at least five objectives He may want to accomplish in our lives.

First, God can use pain to *develop our faith*. As the saying goes, "No pain, no gain." Just as endurance is developed in a long-distance runner through strenuous exercise, so faith grows through testing (see James 1:2–4).

Second, God can *expose error* through pain. Heat has a way of bringing impurities to the surface, whether they are in our theological understanding or our ethics (1 Cor. 3:13–15).

Third, our relationship with God grows through pain as we *learn obedience*. It is by falling and scraping our knees that we learn to walk safely (see Heb. 5:8).

Fourth, God can use pain to *create humility* in how we relate to others. Our thorns in the flesh have a way of piercing pride and deflating an overblown estimation of ourselves (see 2 Cor. 12:7).

Ultimately, our suffering can *bring glory to God* as we respond with grace. As suggested by the Shorter Westminster Catechism, the chief end of man is to glorify God and enjoy Him forever. God's glory and our highest good form the mountain lake into which the winding tributaries of our pain eventually flow (see 1 Peter 4:16).

Four Ways We Can Encourage the Sufferer

When suffering steamrolls a life, it can leave the person feeling flattened and deflated on the cold, hard concrete. Crushed by the rolling weight of persecution, the Thessalonian believers were like the man in Jesus' parable who was beaten by thieves, robbed, and left for dead. Paul, however, was not like the priest and the Levite, who looked the other way and went about their business. In 2 Thessalonians 2:13–17, he took on the role of the Good Samaritan, attending to his friends in Thessalonica who lay bloodied along life's roadside (see Luke 10:25–37). His approach provides us with a first-aid kit we can use to help those who suffer . . . and to help ourselves when we're the ones who are hurting.

Offer Compassion

To truly help hurting people, we must first "enter into" their pain. We must ask ourselves, What does it feel like to suffer? We must look beyond the circumstances to the heart of the person. Often it's not the pain of the wound but the accompanying indignity that hurts the most. Consider the following scenarios: A friend who once embraced you now shuns you. A vicious rumor about you spreads like a fire in a dry canyon, incinerating your reputation.

You make one mistake, but instead of receiving support and understanding, you are betrayed, stepped on, kicked while down, and tossed aside.

Have you suffered like that? If so, you probably felt isolated and alone. You may have questioned your own worth. You were devastated . . . confused . . . disoriented. What did you need most of all? You needed someone to affirm your dignity as a person and encourage you. You longed for someone to be thankful for you, for someone to show you love. This is the sort of first aid that we must give to others and the kind that Paul administered to the beaten-down Thessalonians.

In the first portion of 2 Thessalonians 2:13, he offered this encouragement:

> But we should always give thanks to God for you,
> brethren beloved by the Lord. . . .

Can you feel his compassion? By giving thanks for the Thessalonian believers, he upheld their dignity. By referring to them as "brethren beloved by the Lord," he affirmed the Lord's love for them and their security within the family of God.

If you are enduring pain and suffering yourself, remember this: In spite of how others treat you, you are "beloved by the Lord." If you're in His family, He'll never slam the door in your face. You may run away like the prodigal son, but God will never disown you. Even in a far country, you can have the assurance that there will always be a place for you and loving arms to embrace you when you return—*always!*

Offer Instruction

Suffering frequently causes disorientation and disillusionment. Suffering believers need instruction to reassure and reorient them, to bring God's promises back into focus. Paul wrote:

> But we should always give thanks to God for you, brethren beloved by the Lord, because God has chosen you from the beginning for salvation through sanctification by the Spirit and faith in the truth. It was for this He called you through our gospel, that you may gain the glory of our Lord Jesus Christ. (vv. 13–14)

39

The truckload of theology freighted away in these two verses helps stabilize the person who is suffering. First, these verses tell the sufferer: "God has chosen you for salvation; you're still in His family even though you may not feel like it." Second, they remind him or her: "God has called *you*. You didn't whistle for help. He did the calling."

Paul's brief but weighty doctrinal points had the effect of a strong anchor on a windblown ship. They stabilized the Thessalonian believers whose faith had been wind-whipped by trials. Good theology has a steadying effect on suffering people who can't see God's hand in the fierce storm. It lifts their focus from the present predicament to the overarching purpose of God—which had its beginnings "in the eternity of the past" and will lead to the "eternity of the future." Theologian John R. W. Stott eloquently wrote:

> In the eternity of the past God chose us to be saved. Then he called us in time, causing us to hear the gospel, believe the truth and be sanctified by the Spirit, with a view to our sharing Christ's glory in the eternity of the future. In a single sentence the apostle's mind sweeps from "the beginning" to "the glory." There is no room in such a conviction for fears about Christian instability. Let the devil mount his fiercest attack on the feeblest saint, let the Antichrist be revealed and the rebellion break out, yet over against the instability of our circumstances and our characters, we set the eternal stability of the purpose of God.[1]

Offer Exhortation

Besides compassion and instruction, hurting people need exhortation. To *exhort* means "to give warnings or advice."[2] In verse 15, Paul encouraged the Thessalonians to persevere:

> So then, brethren, stand firm and hold to the traditions which you were taught, whether by word of mouth or by letter from us. (2 Thess. 2:15)

1. John R. W. Stott, *The Message of Thessalonians: Preparing for the Coming King*, The Bible Speaks Today series (Leicester, England: Inter-Varsity Press, 1991), p. 177.

2. *Merriam-Webster's Collegiate Dictionary*, 10th ed., see "exhort."

Paul's exhortation referred to the situation described earlier in chapter 2. The Thessalonians were shaken from their composure and disturbed by some false information (v. 2), were being deceived (v. 3), and were forgetting some of the teaching Paul had given them earlier (v. 5). False teaching had tossed them about, and shipwreck was imminent unless they took measures to secure their faith.

Two commands formed Paul's exhortation: "stand firm" and "hold to the traditions." Picture a person planting his or her feet in a secure spot with knees bent and shoulders squared in a determined, defensive stance. Then that person stabilizes further by clinging to something fixed. Feet on the ground; hands gripping something solid—the "traditions," Paul said. These are the teachings of Jesus Christ that had been handed down by the apostles. The key to withstanding the onslaught of false teaching was for the Thessalonians to hang on to true teaching.

For us, the command is the same. In times of suffering, nothing is more stabilizing than the truth of Scripture—nothing. Trials pressure us to try something new. We might be drawn toward a new belief, the latest doctrinal twist, or perhaps a self-help program that "guarantees" to make us feel better, but Paul's exhortation for us is to remain stubbornly loyal to the tried-and-true doctrines of the faith. Like Paul, we are to encourage those who suffer by pointing them toward the truth of God's Word.

Offer Intercession

The final two verses of the chapter form a brief prayer on behalf of the Thessalonian believers:

> Now may our Lord Jesus Christ Himself and God our Father, who has loved us and given us eternal comfort and good hope by grace, comfort and strengthen your hearts in every good work and word. (vv. 16–17)

Notice what Paul does and doesn't pray for. He prays for God to comfort them, not to circumnavigate the storms for them. He prays for God to strengthen them, not for Him to spare them. Actually, it sounds much like Jesus' prayer in John 17:15: "I do not ask You to take them out of the world, but to keep them from the evil one."

When the storms of life come sweeping over us, we, like the disciples, want calm. Whatever the route, we want to avoid the storms. But in most cases, the most direct route to maturity is through the storms, not around them. Look carefully at the words of God in Isaiah 43:2:

> "When you pass through the waters, I will be
>   with you;
> And through the rivers, they will not overflow you.
> When you walk through the fire, you will not
>   be scorched,
> Nor will the flame burn you."

Notice that the word *through* is used three times in the passage. God does not guarantee us a life full of sunshine and free from storms. What He does guarantee, however, is His loving care over us as we go *through* those times. "For I am the Lord your God. . . . you are precious in My sight. . . . I love you" (Isa. 43:3–4).

The calm in the storm is God's watchful eye. If you are suffering today, are you focusing on the wind and the waves, or are you making eye contact with the One who considers you precious in His sight? Your focus will determine whether you sink in your circumstances or walk above them (see Matt. 14:29–30). If someone you know is suffering, offer prayerful intercession for them and remind them of these truths.

Three Benefits from Suffering

Why does God allow pain in our lives? That's a question we have all asked at one time or another. As much as we yearn to make sense of our suffering, God doesn't always give us the answers we want to hear. Often silence is the only response we get, despite our desperate pleadings. Part of the faith-building process of trials is learning to let go of the need to know why and focusing on the good that difficult experiences can produce in us.

In 2 Corinthians 1, Paul lists three benefits reserved for those who make it through suffering's collision course. The first benefit is *the ability to comfort others*:

> Blessed be the God and Father of our Lord Jesus Christ, the Father of mercies and God of all comfort, who comforts us in all our affliction so that we will be able to comfort those who are in any affliction with the comfort with which we ourselves are comforted by God. (vv. 3–4)

42

The second benefit is *a dependence on God*:

> For we do not want you to be unaware, brethren, of our affliction which came to us in Asia, that we were burdened excessively, beyond our strength, so that we despaired even of life; indeed, we had the sentence of death within ourselves so that we would not trust in ourselves, but in God who raises the dead. . . . (vv. 8–9)

The third benefit is *learning to give thanks in everything*:

> . . . who delivered us from so great a peril of death, and will deliver us, He on whom we have set our hope. And He will yet deliver us, you also joining in helping us through your prayers, so that thanks may be given by many persons on our behalf for the favor bestowed on us through the prayers of many. (vv. 10–11)

Like food, clothing, and shelter, these verses address our basic needs during suffering. They point to the God who can leave us warmed and filled. In Him, we find a light in the darkness that leads us into a harbor of peace that shelters us from the storms. These verses reveal not only the path where our suffering leads but also the tender hand of God who leads us.

🌸 *Living Insights*

With the advent of high technology, scientists can measure the intensity of the pain we feel. They can determine that a toothache hurts more than a hangnail or a broken arm more than a skinned elbow. They have concluded that two of the most painful life experiences are giving birth and passing a kidney stone. From a purely physical point of view, both hurt with great intensity. However, the two are different in their results. One is a natural fruition of the body processes; the other is a malfunction of the body processes. One is purposeful suffering; the other, pointless suffering.

The pain of giving birth is a creative pain—one that has meaning and can produce life. The pain of passing a kidney stone, on the other hand, leads only to a return to the status quo of physical functions. This is why a person who passes a kidney stone never

43

wants to go through the experience again, while many women who have given birth anticipate the time when they will be able to have their next baby (compare John 16:21).

Although you may never know all the purposes for the pain in your life, take a few moments now to think about the fruit that has come from your suffering. In the following space, list a particular hardship you endured and the good that God redeemed from it.

_____

_____

_____

_____

Going through painful experiences in life can be like walking barefooted through the dark and stubbing your toe on a sharp corner. In spite of the fact that we know God has purposefully arranged the furniture in our lives, we still have a tendency to want to curse the darkness. But the next time life jams your toe or scrapes a shin, try turning on a light instead. Try turning to His Word.

> Your word is a lamp to my feet
> And a light to my path. (Ps. 119:105)

Read through the following verses, and choose one to carry with you as a flashlight the next time you're in pain and need the light of God's Word to guide you through the dark valleys.

> Psalm 23:4
> Psalm 37:24
> Psalm 73:21–23
> Matthew 28:20
> Hebrews 13:5

Small Group Insights

The book *A Severe Mercy* describes the magnificent love story of Sheldon Vanauken and his wife, Davy, and the depths of their pain as they attempt to cope with Davy's eventually fatal illness. After her death, Sheldon embarks on an intense experience of grief—to find its meaning, to taste it, and to learn the lessons that sorrow had to teach him. He comes to terms with his loss as he ponders God's goodness and mercy in allowing trials that bring maturity and growth.

Have you ever experienced what you would call "severe mercy" from the hand of God? If so, how? Share your answer with your small group.

_____

_____

_____

How has God used difficult experiences to change you? How did those around you react to your circumstances?

_____

_____

_____

What lessons has sorrow taught you about yourself? About God?

_____

_____

_____

How can you reach out to others who are suffering? Name one person you know who is going through a difficult time. Then list a specific way that you or your group can minister to him or her this week.

_____

_____

_____

Chapter 6

CORDS THAT HOLD PASTORS AND FLOCKS TOGETHER

2 Thessalonians 3:1–5

Pastors have been compared to shepherds since the beginning of the church. The apostle Peter encouraged the church elders to "shepherd the flock of God among you" (1 Peter 5:2). The word *pastor* itself comes from a Latin word that means "herdsman."[1] Just as shepherds guide and tenderly care for their flocks, so pastors lead and serve the needs of their congregation.

However, relationships between pastors and flocks are not always as serene as the pastoral image might imply.

Sheep sometimes stray and sometimes bleat behind the shepherd's back. Pastors sometimes fight with the sheep and sometimes flee altogether. Often fed up with the flock and in search of greener pastures, pastors vacate pulpits on an average of once every three years.

One or two sheep with a little "goat" in them can butt heads often enough with the pastor to make his ministry miserable. The lingering, unresolved personality conflicts can drain both his emotions and his energy. Sometimes, too, the sheep can crowd the shepherd to such an extent that his personal time for study and growth are eaten away. Gradually, his life and teaching lose their cutting edge, growing dull and ineffective. Also, out of either insecurity or a desire to set a sterling example, some pastors are reluctant to be real, vulnerable, and open.

All pastors have needs. Underneath the ministerial garb, they are sheep like everyone else. They hurt when bitten, fight or run when threatened, and shiver in the wind when shorn. In 2 Thessalonians 3:1–5, Paul reveals a lot about himself as a pastor and about his relationship to the flock at Thessalonica. In doing so, he indirectly instructs us in strengthening the pastor-flock relationship.

Strengthening the Pastor-Flock Relationship: The Pastor

Strengthening church relationships begins with the pastor. Four responsibilities for pastors emerge from verses 1–3.

1. *Merriam-Webster's Collegiate Dictionary*, 10th ed., see "pastor."

Admission of Need

Paul opened chapter 3 of his letter by making a personal request on behalf of himself and his fellow ministers: "Finally, brethren, pray for us" (v. 1a). Without self-consciousness or shame, Paul solicited the sheep to share in his burden through prayer.

How often we rob people of the joy of sharing our pain and shouldering our burdens! Whether through insecurity or self-sufficiency, we create an unreal and unattainable image of the Christian experience. People may bow before the image, but a distance will always exist there.

As we skim the New Testament, we find many examples of Paul requesting prayer. He asked the Roman believers (Rom. 15:30), the Ephesian believers (Eph. 6:19), the Colossian believers (Col. 4:3), and earlier he had asked the Thessalonian believers (1 Thess. 5:25) to pray for him. He also encouraged individuals like Philemon to pray for him (Philem. 22).

The New Testament picture of Paul is not an eight-by-ten-inch glossy portrait of self-assurance. Rather, it is one of dependency—not only on God, but on the people of God. And that dependency is reflected in Paul's need for prayer.

Declaration of Objective

Paul asked his readers to pray "that the word of the Lord will spread rapidly and be glorified" (2 Thess. 3:1b). With this request came an insight into Paul's objective for ministry—that the Gospel would "spread rapidly." Literally, the Greek word used here means "run."[2] Paul likened the Gospel message to an Olympic runner racing across the countryside. He prayed that, as the word of the Lord entered a town, crowds would line the streets and cheer it on to the next town, where it would receive the same hero's welcome. Paul wanted none of the fame for himself. All of it was for the Lord and the spread of His Good News of salvation.

At the end of verse 1, notice how Paul affirmed his flock: "Pray that the word of the Lord will spread rapidly and be glorified, just as it did also with you." As a model pastor, Paul constantly gave his flock words of positive affirmation (see 1 Thess. 1:6–8; 2:13). He praised the Thessalonian believers for the way they received the Gospel. Few things are more encouraging to a pastor than the

---

2. G. Abbott-Smith, *A Manual Greek Lexicon of the New Testament,* 3d ed. (The University Press, Aberdeen, Scotland, for T. & T. Clark, Edinburgh, Scotland, 1937), p. 450.

positive response of the flock to the declaration of God's Word. And few things are more discouraging than to feel that the seed sown has fallen on hardened hearts or deaf ears.

Recognition of Human Opposition

When doors begin to open for the Gospel, all sorts of accompanying vermin seem to crowd around the entrance. Paul wrote in his letter to the Corinthians, "For a wide door for effective service has opened to me, and there are many adversaries" (1 Cor. 16:9). Apparently, this opposition was happening throughout Paul's travels. He mentioned it in his prayer request to the Thessalonians:

> [Pray] that we will be rescued from perverse and evil men; for not all have faith. (2 Thess. 3:2)

Corrupt adversaries dogged Paul's heels. The Greek text has a definite article before the word *perverse*, indicating that he probably had specific men in mind. Paul boldly names two such enemies in 1 Timothy 1:18–20: Hymenaeus and Alexander. Again, in 2 Timothy 4:14, Paul refers to Alexander as having done him "much harm."

A pastor needs to be realistic in recognizing that he will not only face opposition, but *aggressive* opposition. The sharp-toothed jaws of a relentless wolf can give a shepherd many a sleepless night. Because of this, the pastor needs to solicit prayer from the church.

Proclamation of God's Faithfulness

On the positive side, the Lord, as the ultimate Shepherd, watches over the entire flock—both pastor and parish. Paul knew this and quieted every anxious thought with the words:

> But the Lord is faithful, and He will strengthen and protect you from the evil one. (2 Thess. 3:3)

God is faithful. What a comforting contrast to the enemies mentioned in verse 2 who have no faith. "The faithlessness of human beings cannot possibly overturn the faithfulness of God," wrote theologian John R. W. Stott. He continued:

> True, there was opposition from "evil men" (2), and behind them from "the evil one" himself (3). True also, they were engaged in spiritual warfare and so needed spiritual weapons: Paul had to preach and the Thessalonians had to pray. Yet behind his

preaching and their prayers stood the faithful Lord himself, who watches over his word, and who confirms it by his Spirit in the hearers' hearts, so that it works in them effectively. (1 Thess. 1:5; 2:13)[3]

When evil adversaries breathe down your neck, driven by the Evil One himself, don't veer off course. God is faithful. Behind what may seem to be a curtain of darkness is your faithful Good Shepherd who is keeping watch (see John 10:12–14). His mark is the standard against which all people, including your adversaries, must one day measure themselves. Keep yourself on His course, and He will keep you in His care.

Strengthening the Pastor-Flock Relationship: The Flock

With the change in pronouns from "us" and "we" (vv. 1–2) to "you" and "your" (vv. 3–5), Paul's emphasis changes from pastor to flock.

Protection from Attack

The doctrine of God's faithfulness forms a watershed in Paul's thought. Paul's affirmation, "the Lord is faithful," is essential to his message. Stott said of this faithfulness, "It looks back to the spread of the word and on to the strengthening of the church. God will not allow either his word or his church to fail."[4]

Paul assured the flock that the Lord would "strengthen and protect" them from the "evil one" (v. 3b). The Greek word for "strengthen," *sterizo*, means "to confirm, establish."[5] Paul had sent Timothy to establish the Thessalonian believers, just as a builder might firm up a weak foundation to stand against high winds (see 1 Thess. 3:2–3). Earlier Paul prayed that the Lord Himself would establish their hearts (2 Thess. 2:16–17), and now he expresses complete confidence in the faithfulness of God: "He *will establish you.*"

The Lord will protect His flock. After all, the church belongs to Him (see Matt. 16:18). He will strengthen His people from within and protect them from without. God faithfully does all this so that we will be shielded from our ultimate adversary, the Evil

3. John R. W. Stott, *The Message of Thessalonians: Preparing for the Coming King*, The Bible Speaks Today series (Leicester, England: InterVarsity Press, 1991), p. 186.

4. Stott, *The Message of Thessalonians*, p. 186.

5. Abbott-Smith, *A Manual Greek Lexicon of the New Testament*, p. 445.

One, who roams about the earth seeking whom he may devour (1 Pet. 5:8).

Cooperation with the Leadership

God's faithfulness to His people should inspire a response. In 2 Thessalonians 3:4, Paul expressed confidence that his readers would do what was right and cooperate with the apostolic leadership:

> We have confidence in the Lord concerning you, that you are doing and will continue to do what we command.

It's one thing to listen to good teaching; it's another thing to respond to the Scriptures when they confront our lifestyle. God wants us to be *doers* of the Word (see James 1:22). God desires us to display not only orthodox theology but also orthodox morality. Immorality eats away at the fiber of a congregation. It grows in the clandestine closets of a church, silent and undetected, like mildew. In the damp, sheltered darkness, it flourishes. Before long, the fabric of the church is like a handful of filthy rags—a far cry from the "fine linen, bright and clean" of a bride waiting for her groom (Rev. 19:7–8). Paul had confidence that the Thessalonian believers were living up to the high standards of godly living.

Cultivation of Love for God

Realizing the flock's need to depend on its divine Shepherd for its life, Paul prayed a benediction upon his readers: "May the Lord direct your hearts into the love of God" (2 Thess. 3:5a). The key to Christian stability is the love of God. John Stott observed:

> Three times Paul alludes to it in 2 Thessalonians 2 and 3. . . . Behind God's election, call and gifts there lies God's love. That God is love, that he has set his love upon us, that he loves us still, and that his love will never let us go, is the foundation not only of all reality, but of Christian confidence and Christian stability too. Our stability is not only im-possible, but actually inconceivable, apart from the steadfastness of the love of God.[6]

---

6. Stott, *The Message of Thessalonians*, p. 180.

During intense storms of affliction, God's love for us is like an anchor, and our love for Him is the line that keeps us connected to it. Both His love for us and our love for Him are necessary, and both are implied in Paul's prayer.

Determination to Endure for Christ

Paul prayed that the Lord would direct the Thessalonians' hearts into the love of God "and into the steadfastness of Christ," who is our model of endurance (v. 5b). *Steadfastness* is not a word we use often in everyday conversation, but we can think of it as just old-fashioned "stick-to-it-iveness." Eugene Peterson's book on steady discipleship in an instant culture expresses the idea well, calling it "a long obedience in the same direction."[7]

We all aspire to "long obedience," yet our experience often reflects short bursts of obedience in different directions, which leads to instability. True perseverance levels out our roller-coaster emotions. We learn to obey whether or not we feel like it. Convenience and ease don't matter. With the steadfastness of Christ, we can stay fixed on the target of doing God's will regardless of the consequences.

Some Secrets for Long-Term Ministries

Several principles leap off the page in 2 Thessalonians 3:1–5. These principles are crucial for lasting ministries.

Pastors and flocks must commit to praying for one another. Intercessory prayer unifies the church and keeps the leaders humble and vulnerable.

Pastors and flocks must agree on essentials. Just as a crew must agree on certain principles of navigation for the ship to steer a straight course, so the church must agree on certain points of doctrine (such as the way of salvation, the deity of Christ, and the authority of Scripture) to keep the ministry heading in the same direction.

Pastors and flocks must be involved in ministry together. Have you ever seen carpenters building a house with one person working in the hot sun while the rest of the crew relaxes in the shade? Houses aren't built that way . . . and neither are ministries. Pastors and church members must toil together.

Pastors and flocks need a humble acknowledgment of need. The clergy and laity stand on equal ground before God. Neither is above

7. Eugene H. Peterson, A Long Obedience in the Same Direction: Discipleship in an Instant Society (Downers Grove, Ill.: InterVarsity Press, 1980).

reproof, and both need to draw strength from the Lord. When both pastors and their congregations humble themselves and admit their need for God, He blesses and uses them in a mighty way to impact their churches, their communities, and their world.

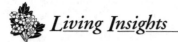 *Living Insights*

The Lord's faithfulness is reflected in the fact that He intercedes for us. Before He went to the cross, Jesus prayed to the Father for our protection: "I do not ask You to take them out of the world, but to keep them from the evil one" (John 17:15).

We have a superhuman adversary in Satan—aggressive, ravenous, cunning—but we have a stronger ally: "Greater is He who is in you than he who is in the world" (1 John 4:4b).

Have the Devil's wolves been hounding you lately? Perhaps discouragement, doubt, fear, and worry have circled around you, tearing at the fabric of your faith. How does Paul's reminder of God's faithfulness in this passage strengthen your spirit?

_____

_____

_____

_____

Just as the stability of a house lies in its foundation, the stability of our faith is found not in us but in the Person our faith is built upon. Take a few moments as you close this chapter to prayerfully meditate on the Lord and His love for you. Record the insights that your current trials may be revealing about Him.

_____

_____

_____

_____

_____

The parable of the Pharisee and the publican, or tax collector, in Luke 18:9–14 vividly illustrates the problems that arise when we compare ourselves to others within the church. Read this parable together and answer the following questions.

To whom was Jesus addressing this parable? What were His purposes for telling it? How do you think it affected the listeners?

_____

_____

_____

How did the Pharisee characterize himself? The tax collector? With which person in this parable do you identify the most?

_____

_____

_____

How do Christians today compare themselves to others? Name some ways that you can reach out to others who might not feel accepted in your church, workplace, or community.

_____

_____

Conclude your time together by praying Paul's prayer in 2 Thessalonians 3:1–5 for your church and its pastors. Pray for God's protection from the Evil One. Express your dependence on God's faithfulness and love.

_____

_____

_____

_____

_____

Chapter 7

BUYING INTO THE VISION
2 Thessalonians 3:6–15

Great leaders have powerful vision. They see the way things are, but they also imagine the way things could be. They skillfully communicate their ideas to others, and people follow them—often sacrificially—because they buy into their vision.

During His ministry, Jesus set forth a vision of the kingdom of God. Everywhere He traveled, He proclaimed "the gospel of the kingdom" (Matt. 4:23). Through His miracles, He offered sips of the coming kingdom—quenching parched lips and whetting people's appetites for a new world free from sin, pain, and death.

When surrounded by the diseased and dying, Jesus healed them. When He encountered the distressed and shepherdless multitudes, He was moved with compassion, and He taught and fed them. He demonstrated forgiveness and love when He touched the heart of an outcast Samaritan woman (John 4:7–29) and when He washed the disciples' dirty feet (13:5–20). Jesus proved His authority as Ruler of the kingdom when He overcame "the ruler of this world" in the wilderness and defeated him at the Cross (see John 12:31; Matt. 4:1–11; Col. 2:13–15).

As Jesus' disciples, we have tasted the life He offers—the eternal, abundant life available to those who submit to the King's authority. We believe in Jesus Christ and His vision for us and our world. But what does the Lord expect from us now? What are the practical implications of embracing His vision?

Involvement in the Kingdom

Vision *acceptance* implies vision *involvement*. Notice the variety of ways that the Scriptures teach us to put our faith into action. Jesus instructed us to get involved in His kingdom ministry by "investing our talents"—in other words, by making good use of the abilities that He has given us (see Matt. 25:14–30). The apostle Paul taught that we are to abound in the work of the Lord, knowing that our toil won't be in vain (1 Cor. 15:58). Paul used an agricultural analogy, encouraging us to sow in order to reap (Gal. 6:6–9). He also drew an illustration from athletics, exhorting us to "fight the good fight of faith" (1 Tim. 6:11–12), to run to win, and to compete using self-control in order to gain an imperishable reward (1 Cor. 9:24–27). We are to be fervent and active in our love for one another (1 Pet. 4:7–11), as well as alert and resistant to Satan's schemes. Finally, we are to throw ourselves into our work "heartily" as unto the Lord (Col. 3:23).

The verbs of Christian involvement are vivid and active: *invest, abound, fight, run, compete, resist, work.* But unfortunately, we might describe the involvement of many believers as more vague than vivid . . . more passive than active.

A Strong Exhortation to All Christians

It's comfortable to sit back with our feet on our desks in the Christian life. It's easy for us to "go with the flow," remaining neutral on matters that call for action, indecisive regarding moral issues, and irresponsible and lazy when it comes to the workload. But God calls us to step up and get involved!

Some of the Thessalonian believers used the Lord's return as an excuse for inactivity (see 2 Thess. 3:6–15). They believed in the coming kingdom, but they didn't fully comprehend the implications of God's vision for their daily lives. Because they thought Christ's return would be soon, they reasoned that it was futile to work and make long-term plans. The result was that these people began sponging off of wealthier church members, becoming a class of Christian beggars. Paul faced this deplorable situation head-on.

The Command

Paul's exhortation to those living irresponsibly was strong and forthright:

> Now we command you, brethren, in the name of our Lord Jesus Christ, that you keep away from every brother who leads an unruly life and not according to the tradition which you received from us. (2 Thess. 3:6)

Paul referred to these irresponsible believers as those who led "unruly" lives. According to one lexicon, the Greek term for *unruly* means "out of order, out of place . . . [and was frequently used] of soldiers not keeping the ranks or an army in disarray."[1]

1. G. Abbott-Smith, *A Manual Greek Lexicon of the New Testament*, 3d ed. (The University Press, Aberdeen, Scotland, for T. & T. Clark, Edinburgh, Scotland, 1937), p. 67.

Maybe Paul had in mind an image of soldiers who marched to their own beat, who stayed in bed while everyone else reported for duty, who didn't pull their own weight, and who expected others to take care of the duties they neglected.

Or maybe Paul had in mind another image associated with the Greek word *unruly*, which was also used "of truancy on the part of an apprentice."[2] This word picture describes a young person running off to have fun rather than reporting to school. Some of the Thessalonian believers had become truant. Lazy and irresponsible, they were like kids playing hooky from school, kids who were concerned only with their immediate interests and pleasures rather than doing the hard work of learning and growing.

God commands us to "keep away"—to avoid, move away, or withdraw—from such people. An example of this form of discipline can be found in Romans 16:17–19, in which Paul warned the believers in Rome to stay away from false teachers who were "slaves . . . of their own appetites" and who deceived others "by their smooth and flattering speech." In Thessalonica, the threat wasn't posed by smooth-talking shysters but chattering sluggards, yet the response was the same: Stay away from them!

The Example

Whose example were the Thessalonian believers to follow? Paul offered himself and his colleagues as models of Christian responsibility:

> For you yourselves know how you ought to follow our example, because we did not act in an undisciplined manner[3] among you, nor did we eat anyone's bread without paying for it, but with labor and hardship we kept working night and day so that we might not be a burden to any of you; not because we do not have the right to this, but in order to offer ourselves as a model for you, so that you would follow our example. For even when we were with you, we used to give you this order: if anyone is not willing to work, then he is not to eat, either. (2 Thess. 3:7–10)

2. Abbott-Smith, *A Manual Greek Lexicon of the New Testament*, p. 66.

3. The Greek word translated "did not act in an undisciplined manner" is the verb form of the same word that Paul used in verse 6, *unruly*. Paul was saying that he was the direct opposite of the irresponsible believers who had fallen out of rank in the church.

During his visit to Thessalonica, Paul worked day and night so as not to be a burden to the new converts (see also 1 Thess. 2:9). He paid his own way and picked up his own tab, even though Jesus had said that preachers might rightfully obtain their livelihood from the work of the Gospel (1 Cor. 9:14). Paul pointed out his right as an apostle to expect support, but he willingly forfeited that right for the sake of setting an example (see also 1 Cor. 9:1–14).

Paul followed his own rule of thumb: "If anyone is not willing to work, then he is not to eat, either." This maxim does not apply to those who *can't* work, but to those who *refuse* to work. The emphasis is on the will, and the continuous tense suggests a habitual attitude.

The Encouragement

Ironically, the "truants" in the Thessalonian church were not inactive. They were busy, all right . . . being busybodies:

> For we hear that some among you are leading an un-
> disciplined life, doing no work at all, but acting like
> busybodies. Now such persons we command and ex-
> hort in the Lord Jesus Christ to work in quiet fashion
> and eat their own bread. But as for you, brethren,
> do not grow weary of doing good. (2 Thess. 3:11–13)

For the third time in this passage Paul uses the same term, here rendered "undisciplined" (see also vv. 6–7). People who have a lot of spare time and skip out on their responsibilities often resort to idle chatter. In 1 Timothy 5:13, Paul links idleness to being a busybody. A *busybody* is a person who meddles in the lives of others. Busybodies flit from house to house, taking little nectared drops of gossip with them and leaving behind their own residue of irritating pollen.

There's a vast difference between putting your nose in other people's business and putting your heart into their problems. Paul's advice to the Thessalonians here is similar to the advice he gave in his first letter:

> Make it your ambition to lead a quiet life and attend
> to your own business and work with your hands, just
> as we commanded you. (1 Thess. 4:11)

He concluded his comments to the dutiful troops with the follow-ing: "Do not grow weary of doing good." The words are reminiscent of those written to the Galatians: "Let us not lose heart in doing good, for in due time we will reap if we do not grow weary" (Gal. 6:9).

The doctrine of the Lord's return should not discourage us from working but strengthen us; it should not make us idle but patient and more focused on our priorities.

The Admonition

Verses 14–15 bring Paul's message full circle:

> If anyone does not obey our instruction in this letter, take special note of that person and do not associate with him, so that he will be put to shame. Yet do not regard him as an enemy, but admonish him as a brother.

Paul repeats his command for us not to associate with those who fall out of the ranks. If we do, we'll reward their foolishness with our attention, and we'll get out of step as well! He reminds us to "admonish" the offender as a "brother," not treat him "as an enemy." With a brother, the ultimate goal is restoration.

There's a fine line between putting a person to shame ("You have done a bad thing") and shaming a person ("You're a bad person"). When we're put to shame, we feel sorry for our sins and the hurt they cause others, and we yearn to make things right again. Shaming a person, however, leaves no room for restoration. It is a life sentence that can never be appealed or overturned. Paul urges us to treat one another like family members—with our arms wide open when our brother or sister comes back home.

Practical Implications

Have you bought into Christ's vision for your life and for the world? If so, how involved are you in making that vision a reality? The vision is specific—to "make disciples of all the nations" (Matt. 28:19)—but your involvement can take various forms depending on the abilities God has given you. In the church and community, your family and your neighborhood, you can carry on the ministry and vision of Jesus.

To be only an observer in the Christian life, detached and distant, is to take the safe seat—like watching a war from an easy chair in front of the television. Uncommitted and uninvolved believers take the path of least resistance. They live routine, predictable, status quo lives—lives of mediocrity.

The exhilarating times occur in the climb upward. Is it an arduous journey? Most certainly. Perilous? On occasion. And yes, you'll get winded and weary along the way, but wait until you see the view from the peak of Christian commitment! Someday all Christians will look back on their lives which were traveled on one of two separate roads: either lived heartily for the Lord or only half-heartedly. And depending on which way we choose, we will receive either His reward or an empty hand (Col. 3:23–24; 2 Cor. 5:10; 1 Cor. 3:10–15).

If you've gotten a glimpse of Christ's vision, how can you get involved in working out that vision in your personal life?

_____

_____

_____

In your family life?

_____

_____

In your church?

_____

_____

In your community?

_____

_____

_____

_____

Pick at least one of these ideas and put it into practice this week. Don't stay on the predictable plateau; start climbing those mountains!

Small Group Insights

Sculptor and architect Maya Ying Lin once said, "To fly we have to have resistance."[4] Similarly, in order to soar in our spiritual lives, we must take risks and accept challenges that will make us more mature followers of Christ. Only then will we be able to live as abundantly as God intended.

What resistance have you faced as an individual? As a group? How has this helped you to mature in your faith?

_____

_____

_____

_____

_____

What is your specific contribution to your small group? Your family? Your circle of friends? Your work environment? What steps can you take to more actively minister to those in your sphere of influence?

_____

_____

_____

_____

_____

4. Maya Ying Lin, at http://creativequotations.com/one/1621.htm, accessed on June 19, 2002.

Name some people whom you consider to be "visionaries." How do these people approach life? How do their attitudes and actions differ from those of others you know? How do these visionaries impact their surroundings?

_____

_____

_____

_____

_____

As a follower of Jesus Christ, how would you like to be characterized? (For instance, you may want to be bold in sharing the Gospel, compassionate, disciplined, etc.) What can you do to make these attributes more of a part of your life?

_____

_____

_____

_____

_____

Chapter 8

YOUR DISTINGUISHING MARK
2 Thessalonians 3:16–18

What's in a name? Sometimes everything. Reputations are attached to our names, as well as expectations. Perhaps when you were younger and more rambunctious, you recall your parents giving a warning that went something like this: "Remember who you are. You're a _____ (fill in your family name). Conduct yourself accordingly!"

Reminding yourself of who you are can keep you on the straight path when you're tempted to stray. It can also bring you comfort when you hurt. Think of the name you bear if you've placed your faith in Jesus Christ as your Savior. You're a "Christian," which means "one who belongs to Christ." What a precious reassurance when you feel wounded and harassed like the Thessalonian believers! You don't belong to this world and its hateful ways; you belong to Christ, who has your life in His hands. You're a *Christian*!

According to 2 Corinthians 3:3, not only do you belong to Christ, but you are also "a letter of Christ." Perhaps you've never considered that title before. Christ claims you as His own, so your actions should reflect His character. In a very real sense, you are the pen and ink that communicate Christ to the world.

We've been studying a letter from Paul to the Thessalonians, so it's fitting to focus on our lives as being living letters. Let's take a closer look at 2 Corinthians 3:3 and explore what's in the title "letters of Christ."

On Being "Letters of Christ"

What exactly does it mean to be "letters of Christ"? This reference appears in the context of a debate about Paul's authority as an apostle and teacher. In Paul's day, many traveling preachers, evangelists, and prophets circulated throughout Asia Minor. To establish their credentials as authentic ministers of the Gospel, they carried letters of reference with them. However, the charlatans did this as well. In fact, these imposters were known for their lengthy resumes and numerous letters of reference that supposedly gave them the authority to speak for God.

In 2 Corinthians 3:1, Paul asked the following rhetorical question regarding whether having a letter like this was necessary for him:

> Are we beginning to commend ourselves again?
> Or do we need, as some, letters of commendation
> to you or from you?

In verses 2–3, he responded to his own question:

> You are our letter, written in our hearts, known and
> read by all men; being manifested that you are a
> letter of Christ, cared for by us, written not with ink
> but with the Spirit of the living God, not on tablets
> of stone but on tablets of human hearts.

Paul didn't need written references because the Corinthian believers themselves were proof of Paul's ministry. More importantly, they were proof of Christ's ministry, which was the real source of their transformation.

Every Christian is a *living* letter—not written with ink or etched on tablets of stone, but a *public* letter on open display. And the good news is this: you don't have to preach! All you have to do is live—freely, purely, robustly—as an authentic representative of the King. Wherever you live, wherever you work, wherever you play, you are a living letter of the person of Christ.

A Fitting Conclusion

As living letters, we reflect the Lord—from the truth of His words to the grace of His penmanship. Like handwriting fills a page, Jesus fills us. Although people cannot see the Author, they can see His words and feel their impact. They can touch the pages of our lives and feel His heartbeat, His presence. And His presence in our lives is never as visible as when we demonstrate peace in all our circumstances.

The Believer's Peace and the Lord's Presence

Note Paul's final words to the Thessalonians:

> Now may the Lord of peace Himself continually
> grant you peace in every circumstance. The Lord be
> with you all! (2 Thess. 3:16)

Christ's promise of peace to His disciples forms the basis for

Paul's assurance to the Thessalonians. Before He died, the Prince of Peace Himself comforted His disciples with these words:

> "Peace I leave with you; My peace I give to you; not as the world gives do I give to you. Do not let your heart be troubled, nor let it be fearful." (John 14:27)

Even in their crucible of suffering, the Thessalonian believers had full access to the presence of Christ and, through His presence, His peace. The same peace that Christ experienced on His dark journey to the cross, He offers to His followers in their own pathways of pain. Demonstrating the peace of Christ during suffering stands out like bold print on a page, drawing the eyes of all who examine our lives. This peace provides bold proof of the Author of our faith.

Christ's peace is important to us both personally and interpersonally. In his subsequent letter to the Colossians, Paul wrote: "Let the peace of Christ rule in your hearts" (Col. 3:15a). The context was the theme of "unity in the church." Paul urged the believers to display compassion, kindness, humility, gentleness, and patience toward each other (see v. 12). He encouraged them to forgive one another and to show love, "which is the perfect bond of unity" (v. 14b).

Into this arena of thought, Paul added the command to let the peace of Christ "rule in your hearts." This is the only time in all the New Testament where the original word translated *rule* appears. It means "to act as umpire . . . to arbitrate, decide."[1] Peace is the referee over conflicts within the Body of Christ.

The volatile conflict in the Thessalonian body regarding the lazy Christians who had quit working to wait for the Lord could have splintered the church with explosive arguments and insults. When Paul referred to the Lord granting them peace "in every circumstance" (see 2 Thess. 3:16a), surely he had in mind this powder-keg situation.

In the Thessalonian conflict, Christ's peace was like an arbiter or referee that brought rule and order. And His peace can bring calm and control to our conflicts as well.

The Apostle's Mark

Up to this point, Paul used an *amanuensis*, a secretary who took dictation, to write his letter. But when he came to his concluding

---

1. G. Abbott-Smith, *A Manual Greek Lexicon of the New Testament*, 3d ed. (The University Press, Aberdeen, Scotland, for T. & T. Clark, Edinburgh, Scotland, 1937), p. 85.

remarks, he took the pen to write in his own hand:

> I, Paul, write this greeting with my own hand,
> and this is a distinguishing mark in every letter; this
> is the way I write. (2 Thess. 3:17)

In doing so, Paul gave the letter an indisputable mark of genuineness. This ancient procedure of writing autographic conclusions to dictated letters gave proof of the letter's authenticity. The custom is similar to how we might sign our name or jot down a short personal note at the end of a letter typewritten by a secretary or stenographer.

The Lord's Grace

We, as living letters, have the "distinguishing mark" of Jesus Christ. Like the distinctive handwriting on the Declaration of Independence, the Lord puts His "John Hancock" on our lives. That distinguishing mark is God's grace. And it is with this thought that Paul concludes the letter: "The grace of our Lord Jesus Christ be with you all!" (v. 18). It is the quality of graciousness that transforms our living letters into more treasured correspondence—*love* letters.

Concluding Thought

Let's close our study by pondering the question, What distinguishing mark has the Lord left on our lives? There are no clones in the body of Christ. No two believers are exactly alike. God has graced each of us with our own unique qualities and abilities. What can *you* contribute to the body of Christ? Perhaps by exercising your spiritual gift of teaching, serving, evangelizing, or showing mercy, you can leave your distinguishing mark on others' lives . . . the signature of Christ!

Living Insights

Letters come in all shapes and sizes, printed in various fonts and formats. On any given day, we may receive a visually inviting postcard from a vacationing friend as well as mass-produced form letters from some impersonal computer. Our letters may be personally addressed and postmarked, or they may have been bulk mailed with the designation "Occupant." The greetings may begin with a warm "Dearest" or a cold "To Whom it May Concern."

Certainly, we've all received junk mail which we've tossed unopened into the trash. It may have been stamped "Urgent" in bold block letters, but we automatically realized it to be trivial, having only an incidental claim on our lives.

How about your living letter? Is it read eagerly? Is it warm and inviting or cold and impersonal?

Take a few moments to thumb back through this study guide, and as you review, be on the lookout for the main principles that the Lord has taught you. Write down an application from each chapter that you can inscribe into your living letter.

"Affirming the Afflicted"

_____

_____

_____

_____

"When God Gets the Last Word"

_____

_____

_____

_____

"Praying for Others: A Must"

_____

_____

_____

_____

"Lawlessness: The Man and the Mystery"

_____

_____

_____

_____

"Light for Dark Days"

_____

_____

_____

_____

"Cords That Hold Pastors and Flocks Together"

_____

_____

_____

_____

"Buying into the Vision"

_____

_____

_____

_____

"Your Distinguishing Mark"

_____

_____

_____

_____

Persecution and affliction helped to cultivate consistency, readiness, determination, perseverance, and above all, steadfastness in the spiritual lives of the Thessalonians. In the same way, the Lord uses our difficult circumstances to shape us into more mature believers and make us living letters of Christ. Take heart from Paul's message of affirmation and encouragement. When you face trials and temptations, remember that God loves you and that He is in control of _every_ circumstance!

Small Group Insights

Our names form an integral part of our personal identities. In the same way, our natural talents together with our spiritual gifts help to create our distinguishing marks as followers of Christ. As a group, answer the following questions.

What would you say are your distinguishing marks? What natural talents and abilities has God given you? What personal attributes and characteristics do you model?

_____

_____

_____

What are your spiritual gifts? How do you use these gifts currently? How do they complement your natural gifts and abilities?

_____

_____

_____

How could you utilize your gifts more effectively in your small group, your church, your family, your friendships, your marriage, and your workplace? List several practical ways that you and your group can use your gifts to minister to others this week.

_____

_____

_____

What were the distinguishing marks of the Thessalonians? How did God use their circumstances to make them more mature believers? Within your group, share the insights you have gained from your study of 2 Thessalonians.

_____

_____

_____

BOOKS FOR
PROBING FURTHER

In Paul's second letter to the Thessalonians, we find the believers suffering in chapter 1, shaken from their composure in chapter 2, and slackening in their responsibilities in chapter 3. From our point of view, we might say that the situation in Thessalonica was desperate. But in 2 Thessalonians 1:5–12, Paul offers a heavenly perspective: there is relief awaiting the believers and recompense for the persecutors.

As we look at it from that vantage point, we gain not only perspective, but encouragement to persevere—to walk through the furnace of persecution, over the seas of prophetic error, and around the pitfalls to practical living. Paul's letter allows us to make sense of our suffering, gain stability in doctrinal matters, and become steadfast in principles of responsible living. To help you to gain perspective in your walk, we have listed a few books that we think will prove meaningful and useful.

Key Commentaries on 2 Thessalonians

Morris, Leon. *The First and Second Epistles to the Thessalonians*. Rev. ed. The New International Commentary on the New Testament. Grand Rapids, Mich.: William B. Eerdmans Publishing Co., 1991.

This commentary strikes a good balance between scholarly exactness and popular readability. The technical information is confined to the footnotes, while the body of the text is extremely well written and conservative in its approach.

Stott, John R. W. *The Gospel and the End of Time: The Message of 1 & 2 Thessalonians*. Downers Grove, Ill.: InterVarsity Press, 1991.

Stott's commentary on Thessalonians is a standard. In-depth and pastoral, his examination of the struggles faced by the Thessalonian believers gives us encouragement in the trials we face today.

Key Books on Suffering

Lewis, C. S. *The Problem of Pain*. New York, N.Y.: Macmillan Co., 1970.

This long-recognized classic on the subject of suffering is weighty reading in places but forms a Gibraltar of truth and logic so solid it is virtually immovable.

Key Books on Sound Doctrine

Ryrie, Charles. *Basic Theology*. Wheaton, Ill.: SP Publications, Victor Books, 1986.

Concise and to the point, this excellent summary of Bible doctrine clarifies many of the key aspects of our faith.

Swindoll, Charles R. *Growing Deep in the Christian Life: Essential Truths for Becoming Strong in the Faith*. Grand Rapids, Mich.: Zondervan Publishing House, 1995.

This doctrinal study makes theology not only readable but enjoyable and applicable as well.

Key Books on Sensible Christian Living

Colson, Charles and Nancy Pearcey. *How Now Shall We Live?* Wheaton, Ill.: Tyndale House Publishers, Inc., 1999.

This work addresses how our ideas about the world shape the way we live. The authors assert that Christians are called not only to personal faith but to a biblical worldview that has the power to transform the world.

White, John. *The Fight*. Downers Grove, Ill.: InterVarsity Press, 1978.

In this excellent classic, the author takes us through the basic areas of Christian living with which we wrestle throughout our lives: faith, prayer, temptation, evangelism, guidance, Bible study, fellowship, and work. It is extremely practical and, in places, profound.

Some of the books listed may be out of print and available only through a library. For those currently available, please contact your local Christian bookstore. Books by Charles R. Swindoll may be obtained through the Insight for Living Resource Center, as well as many books by other authors.

Insight for Living also has Bible study guides available on many books of the Bible as well as on a variety of topics, Bible characters, and contemporary issues. For more information, see the ordering instructions that follow and contact the office that serves you.

NOTES

NOTES